Instructor's Manual
and Test Bank
to Accompany

TEN STEPS
to
ADVANCED
READING

John Langan

ATLANTIC CAPE COMMUNITY COLLEGE

TP

Books in the Townsend Press Reading Series:

Groundwork for College Reading
Groundwork for College Reading with Phonics
Ten Steps to Building College Reading Skills
Ten Steps to Improving College Reading Skills
Ten Steps to Advancing College Reading Skills
Ten Steps to Advanced Reading

Books in the Townsend Press Vocabulary Series:

Vocabulary Basics
Groundwork for a Better Vocabulary
Building Vocabulary Skills
Building Vocabulary Skills, Short Version
Improving Vocabulary Skills
Improving Vocabulary Skills, Short Version
Advancing Vocabulary Skills
Advancing Vocabulary Skills, Short Version
Advanced Word Power

Other Reading and Writing Books:

Everyday Heroes
English at Hand
Voices and Values: A Reader for Writers

Supplements Available for Most Books:

Instructor's Edition
Instructor's Manual and Test Bank
Online Exercises

ISBN-13: 978-1-59194-089-0
ISBN-10: 1-59194-089-3

For book orders and requests for desk copies or supplements, contact us in any of the following ways:

By telephone: 1-800-772-6410

By fax: 1-800-225-8894

By e-mail: cs@townsendpress.com

Through our website: www.townsendpress.com

CONTENTS

Note: There are four mastery tests for each skill, supplementing the six mastery tests in the book itself. These tests can be used at a variety of points along the student's path of working through the chapter and the mastery tests in the book.

NOTES FOR INSTRUCTORS

On the first three pages of the Instructor's Edition of *Ten Steps to Advanced Reading*, I list some hints for teaching a reading course and for using the book. I add here some other comments.

Using a Class Contract

In the first class of the semester, I explain to students that I regard the course as a serious, professional relationship between them and me. I say that I want them to sign a professional contract for taking the course. I then pass out a contract for them to read and sign.

In my experience, the contract helps motivate younger students in particular to come to class and to assume responsibility for their own learning. Some of the older students don't need such a contract, but they welcome a clear presentation of basic ground rules regarding attendance and grading in the course.

A copy of the contract appears on pages 6–7; you have permission to modify and use this contract in whatever way you see fit.

Supplements for the Book

There are three supplements for *Ten Steps to Advanced Reading:*

1. An *Instructor's Edition,* which is identical to the student book except that it provides the answers to all of the practices and tests, as well as explanations of the answers.
2. The combined *Instructor's Manual and Test Bank,* which you are now reading.
3. *Online exercises* consisting of three additional mastery tests for each skill plus three combined-skills tests—33 tests in all. These online tests are free for students and instructors using the book and may be accessed at **www.townsendpress.com**.

If you've adopted the book for use in your reading classes, you're entitled to free copies of the two print supplements. Call 1-800-772-6410 or e-mail us at **cs@townsendpress.com** to get them shipped out to you immediately.

A Suggested Syllabus

Weeks 1–10:

One way to begin using *Ten Steps to Advanced Reading* is to have students work through the activities in "How to Become a Better Reader and Thinker" on pages 3–9. Then, as the first homework assignment, ask them to read the essay "A Civil War Soldier's Letter to His Wife" on pages 453–455. Discuss the questions on page 460 in the next class.

I suggest then teaching one chapter a week, following the order in the book. Generally at the end of a chapter I give two mastery tests: one for practice and one that counts for a grade.

I go over the tests in class right after students take them. (I recommend collecting test papers as students finish and distributing them to students in other parts of the room. Some students resist putting X's on a paper that belongs to the person sitting right next to them.) That way students get immediate feedback on how they have done. Also, after class all I need to do is to check the grades quickly and transfer them to my grade book.

As the semester progresses, I use additional mastery tests, every so often, to review previous skills covered in the class.

In the last five weeks, students read two selections a week from Part II of the book. They also do the remaining mastery tests, including some of the tests in this manual, as well as the combined-skills tests in the book and in this manual.

Having done all of the reading of the materials in the book, as well as all of the thinking required to complete the many activities, students are, in my experience, better readers and thinkers. They are better equipped both to handle a standardized reading test at the semester's end and to go on to content courses in their college curriculum.

Suggested Answers to the Discussion Questions

Pages 21–34 in this manual provide suggested answers to the discussion questions that follow each of the twenty readings in Parts I and II of the book. There was simply no room in the Instructor's Edition for this material.

Writing Assignments

Writing and reading are closely related skills: practice at one will make a student better at the other. Also, writing about a selection is an excellent way of thinking about it. For these reasons, three writing assignments are provided (beginning on page 561 of the book) for each of the twenty reading selections in Parts I and II.

If you ask students to write about a selection, I suggest you first have them read the "Brief Guide to Effective Writing" that appears on pages 559–560 of the book.

Teaching Vocabulary

One basic change that I've made in my teaching of reading is that I now directly teach vocabulary. We all know that students don't know enough words. Because they don't, they have trouble understanding what they read, and they're limited in what they can write. (We have all seen how, in standardized reading tests, students are frustrated because they don't know enough of the words in a passage to understand it and to answer comprehension questions about it. And we all know that because of the vocabulary problem, the standardized tests that are intended to measure reading comprehension are often in fact serving as vocabulary tests.)

I teach vocabulary using a words-in-context approach (it is of no value to ask students to memorize isolated lists of vocabulary words). Specifically, I use a book titled *Advanced Word Power*, by Beth Johnson and Susan Gamer. There are thirty chapters in this book, with ten words in each chapter. I do the first chapter in class, so that students understand how to use the pronunciation key for the words and understand just how the chapter works. I then assign two chapters a week for homework.

In class each week, I walk around and check students' books to see that they have worked through the four pages of material for each chapter. (After this quick check, I then return the focus of the class to reading skills.) Every few weeks, I give students one of the several tests that follow each unit of five chapters in the book. My vocabulary syllabus looks like this:

Week 1: Vocabulary chapter 1 covered in class; chapter 2 assigned for homework
Week 2: Vocabulary chapters 3–4 for homework
Week 3: Vocabulary chapters 5–6 for homework plus a test on Unit One in class
Week 4: Vocabulary chapters 7–8 for homework
Week 5: Vocabulary chapters 9–10 for homework plus a test on Unit Two in class
Week 6: Vocabulary chapters 11–12 for homework
Week 7: Vocabulary chapters 13–14 for homework

Week 8: Vocabulary chapters 15–16 for homework plus a test on Unit Three in class
Week 9: Vocabulary chapters 17–18 for homework
Week 10: Vocabulary chapters 19–20 for homework plus a test on Unit Four in class
Week 11: Vocabulary chapters 21–22 for homework
Week 12: Vocabulary chapters 23–24 for homework
Week 13: Vocabulary chapters 25–26 for homework plus a test on Unit Five in class
Week 14: Vocabulary chapters 27–28 for homework
Week 15: Vocabulary chapters 29–30 for homework plus a test on Unit Six in class

The Importance of Continual Reading and Thinking

Continual reading—coupled with thinking about what one has read—is the very heart of a reading class. *One improves the skills of reading and thinking by guided reading and thinking.* This statement is emphasized with good reason. If a teacher is not careful, he or she may play too participatory a role in the classroom, getting more reading and thinking practice than the student does. The teacher should serve as a manager, using the materials in the text to give students the skills practice they need. *Ten Steps to Advanced Reading* helps the teacher ensure that students do a great deal of active reading and thinking in the classroom.

The Importance of Constant Feedback

Along with continual reading, writing, and thinking, it is vital that students get frequent feedback. Here are ways they can secure such feedback:

- Small-group interactions
- Class discussions and reviews
- Short one-on-one sessions with the teacher
- Graded quizzes and tests
- The Limited Answer Key in the back of the book
- The online exercises available at **www.townsendpress.com**

In addition, since instructors using *Ten Steps to Advanced Reading* as a class text are permitted to reproduce any or all parts of this manual, you can selectively hand out copies of answers included here.

All of the exercises in the book are designed to make it easy to give clear and specific feedback. If students are going to learn to read and think more effectively, then they need clear, logical, specific responses to their efforts. This book enables teachers to provide such feedback.

Outlining, Mapping, and Summarizing

To take thoughtful, effective study notes, students need to learn three essential techniques: outlining, mapping, and summarizing. All three techniques often require students to identify the main idea and the major supporting details of a selection. But while educators agree that these three techniques are important for students to learn, they are all too seldom taught.

The book gives students instruction and practice in all three techniques. Passages in the "Supporting Details" and the two "Relationships" chapters, as well as all of the reading selections in Part II, are followed by an outline, a map, or a summary activity. To complete many of these activities, students must look closely at the basic organization of the selection. They must think carefully about what they have read by asking two key questions: "What is the point?" and "What is the support for that point?" As students apply the techniques from one selection to the next and get specific feedback on their efforts, they will develop their ability to think in a clear and logical way.

Readability Levels . . . and Their Limitations

Below are the readability grade levels for the text of the book itself and the twenty reading selections. Because the book has been prepared on a computer, and there are now software programs that determine readability, it has been possible to do a complete readability evaluation for each reading, rather than merely sampling excerpts from the materials.

Please remember, however, that there are limits to the reliability and validity of readability scores. For instance, a readability formula cannot account for such significant factors as student interest, prior knowledge of a subject, the number of examples provided to explain concepts, and the overall clarity and logic of the writing. I respect readability levels, but I also take them with a grain of salt, and I have kept other factors in mind while determining the sequence of readings.

Material	Word Count	Reading Level
Text of *Ten Steps to Advanced Reading*		10
Part I		
1. Getting a Good Night's Sleep	830	11
2. Drug-Altered Consciousness	800	12+
3. "Extra Large, Please"	1636	9
4. Skills of Effective Face-to-Face Conversationalists	1413	11
5. Hoover and Hard Times	1498	12+
6. The Ugly Truth About Beauty	948	8
7. White-Collar Crime	838	11
8. A Vote Against Legalizing Drugs	968	12
9. A Scary Time to Raise a Daughter	947	8
10. Impression Management	796	12
Part II		
1. Personal Conflict Styles	2077	11
2. Cardiovascular Disease Risk Factors	1935	12+
3. Collective Behavior	1359	12+
4. Skills of Effective Face-to-Face Conversationalists	2696	10
5. Sports: Illustrating the Three Perspectives	1924	12+
6. A Civil War Soldier's Letter to His Wife	849	9
7. Single-Sex Schools: An Old Idea Whose Time Has Come	1636	10
8. A King's Folly	2147	8
9. In My Day	2246	10
10. The Spider and the Wasp	2117	11

A Final Note

Writing a book that contains hundreds of explanations and activities is a bit like being in a ball game where one steps up to the batter's box an almost countless number of times. One tries to get as many hits and extra-base hits as possible: to explain every concept so that students really understand it; to provide readings and practices that both interest students and teach the skills. One tries not to hit any foul balls.

Realistically, though, you might find that despite my best efforts, some items may not work. If they don't, and/or if you or your students are confused or uncertain about certain items, let me know so that I can consider making changes in the next printing or revision of the book. Send a note to me at Townsend Press, 439 Kelley Drive, West Berlin, NJ 08091. Alternatively, call Townsend Press at its toll-free number: 1-800-772-6410; send a fax to 1-800-225-8894; or send e-mail to **cs@townsendpress.com**; your comments will be passed on to me. And if you have a question, a Townsend editor will get back to you with an answer very shortly. My thanks in advance for your help in my effort to keep improving the book!

John Langan

A PROFESSIONAL CONTRACT

FOR FIFTEEN WEEKS TOGETHER

between

_____

(Student's name here)

and

_____

(Instructor's name here)

Welcome to *(name of course)* _____. Counting today, we will be spending fifteen weeks together. How successful we are will depend on how well we follow a business contract that I would like you to read and sign, and that I will then sign and return to you. Here are the terms of the contract.

MY ROLE IN THE CONTRACT

My role will be to help you practice and master important reading and writing and thinking and learning skills. I will try to present these communication skills clearly and to give you interesting and worthwhile practice materials. I will conduct this as a skills course—not a lecture course where you could borrow a friend's notes afterward. Typically several skills will be explained briefly in class, and you will then spend most of the class time practicing those skills, making them your own. You will be learning in the best possible way: through doing.

Why learn these skills?

I promise you that the skills will be of real value to you in all the other courses you take in college. They will make you a better reader, writer, thinker, and learner, and they can dramatically increase your chance for success in school.

The skills can be just as valuable for the career work you are likely to do in the future. Consider that America is no longer an industrial society where many people work on farms or in factories. Instead, most jobs now involve providing services or processing information. More than ever, communication skills are the tools of our trade. This course will be concerned directly with helping you learn and strengthen the communication skills that will be vital for job success in the 21st century.

YOUR ROLE IN THE CONTRACT

Experiencing the course

Your role in this contract will be to come to every class and to give a full effort. Much of the value and meaning of this skills course will come from what happens in class, so you must be here on a steady basis. Imagine trying to learn another skill without being present: for example, imagine learning how to drive without the *experience* of actually being in the car and working with the controls and getting feedback from your instructor. How much would you learn about the skill of driving if you relied only on the notes of a classmate? In a similar way, to really learn communication skills, you need direct experience and practice. So if you miss classes, you are in effect missing the course.

Shaping your attitude

Some people start college with a "high-school mindset." They are passive; they do the minimum they need to get by; their attention is elsewhere; they are like the living dead—and the American high-school system (and watching thousands of hours of television) may be to blame. Gradually these people realize that college is not high school: they don't have to be in college, and they are no longer part of the sad game played out in many high schools, where they receive a free ride and promotion no matter how little they do.

If your attitude about learning has been hurt by what happened in high school, then part of your role is to change your attitude. You can do so, and this contract will help.

Understanding sick days and personal days

You should try not to miss *any* classes. But in the professional environment of this class, like in the work world, everyone is entitled to a set number of sick days as well as "personal days"—unexplained absences. In this course, you will have a total of *(insert number)* _____ such days—which can cover such real-world happenings as sickness, car breakdowns, or even the death of someone you know. If you missed more than this amount of time in a real-world job contract, you would be let go. (Only in some extraordinary situation, such as an extended illness confirmed by a doctor's report, might an exception apply.) The professional terms of the work world will apply here: if you miss more than _____ classes, you cannot pass the course.

YOUR ROLE IF YOU MISS CLASS

If you do miss a class, you are responsible for getting the homework for the following week's class. To do so, call a classmate. Write down the names and phone numbers of two people in the room. (For now, use the people sitting on either side of you; you can always change these names later.)

Classmate # 1: *Name* _____   *Phone* _____

Classmate # 2: *Name* _____   *Phone* _____

Note that you **must** turn in all homework assignments, or you **cannot pass the course**.

If a test or tests are given on a day you miss class, you cannot ordinarily make up these tests. Instead, you will receive a grade of M (Missing) for each missed test. When all your grades are averaged at the end of the semester, three M's will be omitted; the rest will convert to zeros.

YOUR COMMITMENT

I've read this contract, and the terms seem fair to me. (I like the fact that this college class is being treated as a professional situation, and I'm learning the ground rules up front.) I accept the responsibility and the challenge to make this course worth my time and money.

_____   _____

Signed by (your name here)   *Date*

_____

Witnessed by the instructor

OR: If you don't want to sign this, please meet with me after this class to talk about why.

ANSWERS TO THE TESTS IN THE BOOK

Answers to the Review and Mastery Tests in Part I

MAIN IDEAS:
Review Test 1
1. point
2. supported
3. topic
4. detail
5. beginning

MAIN IDEAS:
Review Test 2
1. B   6. B
2. C   7. A
3. D   8. A
4. A   9. C
5. C   10. A

MAIN IDEAS:
Mastery Test 1
A. 1. D   **B.** 4. 3
     2. C   5. 2
     3. B

MAIN IDEAS:
Mastery Test 2
A. 1. D   **B.** 4. 1
     2. C   5. 8
     3. A

MAIN IDEAS:
Mastery Test 3
A. 1. C   **B.** 4. 5
     2. D   5. 2
     3. A

MAIN IDEAS:
Mastery Test 4
1. 3
2. 3
3. 1
4. 2
5. 1

MAIN IDEAS:
Mastery Test 5
1. 1
2. 4
3. 3
4. 1
5. 3

MAIN IDEAS:
Mastery Test 6
1. 5
2. 12
3. 3
4. 2
5. 2

SUPPORTING DETAILS:
Review Test 1
1. details
2. details
3. supporting details
4. map
5. summarize

SUPPORTING DETAILS:
Review Test 2
1. A   6. C
2. A   7. D
3. D   8. B
4. A   9. A-1: B
5. C   10. B-2: A

(In the mastery tests, wording of main ideas and supporting details may vary.)

SUPPORTING DETAILS:
Mastery Test 1
A. 1. A
     2. B
     3. C
     4. B
     5. first *or* Another *or* final
B. 6–10. *Main idea:* Advertising fulfills
four basic functions in society.
1. Marketing
2. Educational
3. Economic
4. Social

SUPPORTING DETAILS:
Mastery Test 2
A. 1. A   3. C   5. also
     2. B   4. B
B. 6–10. *Main idea:* Psychologists have
identified four possible outcomes of an
adolescent's identity crisis.
1. Identity achievement: making
    successful personal choices
2. Identity foreclosure: settling for an
    identity provided by others
3. Moratorium: exploring options
    without yet committing to any
4. Identity diffusion: avoiding consider-
    ing options in a conscious way

SUPPORTING DETAILS:
Mastery Test 3
A. 1. A
     2. B
     3. B
     4. A
     5. C
B. 6–10. *Main idea:* Difficult bosses
fall into the following categories.
- Bully
- Jellyfish
- Workaholic
- Aloof

SUPPORTING DETAILS:
Mastery Test 4
A. 1. B
   2. B
   3. A
   4. A
   5. B
   6. To begin with *or* Another *or* final
B. 7–10. *Main idea:* Egocentrism accounts for two fallacies of thought in adolescents.
   1. Imaginary audience—the tendency of teenagers to feel they are constantly being observed and judged by others
   2. Personal fable—adolescents' unrealistic sense of their own uniqueness
      Example: A teenager feels that others couldn't possibly understand the love he or she feels toward a boyfriend or girlfriend.
      Or: A teenager believes he or she is different from other people and won't be touched by the negative things that happen to others.

SUPPORTING DETAILS:
Mastery Test 5
A. 1. B
   2. C
   3. A
   4. A
   5. B
B. 6–10. *Main idea:* American political culture includes the following beliefs.
   • Liberty
   • Self-government
   • Equality
   • Unity

SUPPORTING DETAILS:
Mastery Test 6
A. 1–7. *Main idea:* People use birth control for different reasons.
   1. To provide financial support for children without sacrificing job status
   2. To ensure they will never have children
   Main idea: The choice of birth control method is based on various considerations.
   1. Financial and legal reasons
   2. Availability of professional services
   3. Religious doctrine
B. 8–10.
   • Sanitation
   • Health
   • Increased crime

IMPLIED MAIN IDEAS:
Review Test 1
   1. implied
   2. topic
   3. support
   4. idea *or* point
   5. implied

IMPLIED MAIN IDEAS:
Review Test 2
   1. B   6. C
   2. A   7. D
   3. B   8. A
   4. C   9. B
   5. D   10. B

(In the mastery tests, wording of implied main or central ideas may vary.)

IMPLIED MAIN IDEAS:
Mastery Test 1
   1. D
   2. A
   3. C
   4. C

IMPLIED MAIN IDEAS:
Mastery Test 2
   1. A
   2. D
   3. B
   4. C

IMPLIED MAIN IDEAS:
Mastery Test 3
   1. D
   2. B
   3. A
   4. B

IMPLIED MAIN IDEAS:
Mastery Test 4
   1. D
   2. A
   3. B
   4. Accurately predicting the future is very difficult.

IMPLIED MAIN IDEAS:
Mastery Test 5
   1. C
   2. A
   3. B
   4. Jailing drug dealers and users is not a realistic solution to America's drug problem.

IMPLIED MAIN IDEAS:
Mastery Test 6
   1. C
   2. A
   3. D
   4. Professional boxing is more dangerous than most people realize.

RELATIONSHIPS I:
Review Test 1

1. relationships
2. ideas
3. when *or* at what point
4. organization
5. main idea

RELATIONSHIPS I:
Review Test 2

1. A	6. C
2. D	7. B
3. C	8. B
4. B	9. A
5. A	10. A

RELATIONSHIPS I:
Mastery Test 1

A. 1. B. finally   **B.** 6. first
2. A. also   7. then
3. E. then   8. During
4. C. In addition   9. Finally
5. D. Next   10. B

RELATIONSHIPS I:
Mastery Test 2

A. 1. C. In addition   **B.** 6. first
2. A. before   7. Second
3. D. Later   8. Next
4. B. For one thing   9. Last of all
5. E. second   10. B

RELATIONSHIPS I:
Mastery Test 3

A. 1. B. Another   **B.** 6. first
2. E. Until   7. Next
3. A. also   8. third
4. D. Furthermore   9. Last
5. C. During   10. B

RELATIONSHIPS I:
Mastery Test 4

A. 1. After
2. next
3. then
4. when
5. later
6. B
B. 7. A
8–10. *(Wording of answers may vary.)*
- Fund military projects
- Pay for public works
- Help support the needy

RELATIONSHIPS I:
Mastery Test 5

A. 1. After   4. eventually
2. Then   5. next
3. During   6. B
B. 7. B
8–10. *(Wording of answers may vary.)*
- In the first few months, objects are "out of sight, out of mind."
- By about six months, infants know that objects exist "out there."
- By one year of age, they are aware of the permanence of objects and love peek-a-boo.

RELATIONSHIPS I:
Mastery Test 6

A. 1. A
2–4. *(Wording of answers may vary.)*
- Consistency
- Warm relationship
- Explanation of punishment
B. 5. B
6–10. *(Wording of answers may vary.)*
1. Believe you are not to blame for the abuse.
2. Educate yourself about verbal abuse.
3. Find a support group.
4. Talk to your partner.
5. Consider leaving.

RELATIONSHIPS II:
Review Test 1

1. examples
2. B
3. contrast
4. C
5. C

RELATIONSHIPS II:
Review Test 2

1. C	6. C
2. D	7. A
3. B	8. C
4. A	9. A
5. C	10. D

RELATIONSHIPS II:
Mastery Test 1

A. 1. B. For example   **B.** 6. C
2. C. reason   7. D
3. D. Similarly   8. A
4. E. such as   9. D
5. A. although   10. B

RELATIONSHIPS II:
Mastery Test 2

A. 1. B. For instance   **B.** 6. D
2. C. However   7. B
3. E. reasons   8. A
4. A. effects   9. D
5. D. Likewise   10. C

RELATIONSHIPS II:
Mastery Test 3

A. 1. C   **C.** 5. A
2. like *or* similarly   6. illustration
B. 3. B   **D.** 7. B
4. consequences *or* due to   8. In the same way *or* same

RELATIONSHIPS II:
Mastery Test 4

A. 1. D
2. contrast *or* different *or* Although *or* similar
B. 3. A
4. For instance
C. 5. C
6. on the other hand *or* however
D. 7. B
8. reason *or* Thus

(In Tests 5 and 6, wording of main ideas and supporting details may vary.)

RELATIONSHIPS II:
Mastery Test 5

A. 1. B
2–5. *Main idea:* Due to a number of lifestyle changes, few of today's Americans wear hats.
  1. Change from outdoor culture to indoor culture—hats are no longer needed for protection against heat or cold.
  2. Change from walking or taking public transportation to driving cars—low ceilings in cars make wearing hats awkward.
  3. Change in dress code—hats used to be considered proper but are no longer socially acceptable in many situations.
B. 6. A
7–10.
  • Emotional loneliness—feeling the absence of an intimate attachment figure
    Ex.—Child missing parent; adult missing spouse; individual missing intimate friend; widow missing husband
  • Social loneliness—lacking a sense of being integrated into a community
    Ex.—Young couple moving to a new state, before putting down roots in the community

RELATIONSHIPS II:
Mastery Test 6

A. 1. D (*or* B)
2. different *or* differently *or* however *or* Instead of
3. B (*or* D)
4. affected
5–6.
  1. For women patients, touching was soothing—lowering blood pressure and anxiety.
  2. For men, touching was upsetting—blood pressure and anxiety increased.
B. 7. B
8–10.
  • Abolition of slavery
  • New political majority
  • Ability of citizens to acquire free land

RELATIONSHIPS I and II:
Mastery Test 1

A. 1. E. other
2. D. Later
3. B. due to
4. C. For example
5. A. Conversely
B. 6. D. However
7. A. after
8. B. For instance
9. E. In contrast
10. C. For one thing

RELATIONSHIPS I and II:
Mastery Test 2

A. 1. C
2. For instance *or* include
B. 3. C
4. effects *or* results
C. 5. A
6. in about 1723 *or* in 1750 *or* After *or* On March 5, 1770 *or* then
D. 7. B
8. explanations *or* explanation *or* reason *or* because
E. 9. A
10. Specifically

INFERENCES:
Review Test 1
1. stated
2. inferences
3. D
4. Similes
5. infer

INFERENCES:
Review Test 2
1. A 6. B
2. C 7. C
3. D 8. C
4. B 9. A
5. D 10. A

INFERENCES:
Mastery Test 1
1. B, D
2. A, D
3. A, B
4. A, D
5. A, C

INFERENCES:
Mastery Test 2
A. 1–4. B, C, F, H
B. 5–6. B, C
   7–8. A, D
   9–10. A, D

INFERENCES:
Mastery Test 3
A. 1–4. A, D, G, H
B. 5–10. A, D, E, G, H, J

INFERENCES:
Mastery Test 4
A. 1. B 4. B
   2. C 5. B
   3. A 6. C
B. 7–8. A, C
   9–10. B, D

INFERENCES:
Mastery Test 5
A. 1–5. A, C, D, G, I
B. 6–10. A, B, D, G, J

INFERENCES:
Mastery Test 6
A. 1–5. B, C, E, F, I
B. 6–10. A, D, E, G, I

PURPOSE AND TONE:
Review Test 1
1. inform
2. inform . . . persuade . . . entertain
3. T
4. attitude
5. opposite

PURPOSE AND TONE:
Review Test 2
1. A 6. A
2. C 7. B
3. D 8. C
4. B 9. B
5. D 10. D

PURPOSE AND TONE:
Mastery Test 1
A. 1. I   B. 6. D
   2. I   7. C
   3. P   8. E
   4. E   9. A
   5. P   10. B

PURPOSE AND TONE:
Mastery Test 2
A. 1. I   6. E
   2. P   7. P
   3. E   B. 8. B
   4. I   9. C
   5. P   10. F

PURPOSE AND TONE:
Mastery Test 3
A. 1. I   6. P
   2. P   7. I
   3. E   B. 8. F
   4. P   9. D
   5. E   10. C

PURPOSE AND TONE:
Mastery Test 4
A. 1. I   6. I
   2. P   7. P
   3. E   B. 8. A
   4. P   9. C
   5. E   10. F

PURPOSE AND TONE:
Mastery Test 5
A. 1. C   C. 5. A
   2. B   6. C
B. 3. A   D. 7. B
   4. C   8. C

PURPOSE AND TONE:
Mastery Test 6
A. 1. C   C. 5. B
   2. A   6. A
B. 3. B   D. 7. B
   4. A   8. D

ARGUMENT:
Review Test 1

1. point
2. support
3. complex
4. conclusion
5. adequate

ARGUMENT:
Review Test 2

1. B	6. B
2. D	7. A
3. A	8. B
4. D	9. D
5. D	10. C

ARGUMENT:
Mastery Test 1

A. 1. C   **B.** 5. B
2. D
3. B
4. B

ARGUMENT:
Mastery Test 2

A. 1. A   **B.** 4. D
2. D   5. B
3. C

ARGUMENT:
Mastery Test 3

A. 1. B
2. D
B. 3–5. B, E, F
6–8. B, C, F

ARGUMENT:
Mastery Test 4

A. 1. D
B. 2. D
C. "I agree": A, D, E
"I disagree": B, C, F

ARGUMENT:
Mastery Test 5

A. 1. B
2. D
B. 3–5. B, D, E
C. "I agree": A, B, F
"I disagree": C, D, E

ARGUMENT:
Mastery Test 6

A. 1. B
2. C
B. 3–5. A, D, F
C. "I agree": B, C, E
"I disagree": A, D, F

CRITICAL READING:
Review Test 1

1. opinions
2. facts
3. support (*or* evidence)
4. transfer
5. support (*or* evidence)

CRITICAL READING:
Review Test 2

1. C	6. D
2. D	7. C
3. C	8. D
4. C	9. C
5. A	10. D

CRITICAL READING:
Mastery Test 1

A. 1. O   **B.** 13. F+O
2. F   14. F
3. F   15. F
4. O   16. F+O
5. F   17. F+O
6. O   18. F+O
7. F   19. F
8. F   20. F+O
9. O
10. F
11. O
12. F+O

CRITICAL READING:
Mastery Test 2

A. 1. F   **B.** 13. F+O
2. O   14. F
3. F   15. F
4. F   16. F+O
5. O   17. F+O
6. O   18. F
7. F   19. F
8. F   20. F+O
9. O
10. F
11. O
12. F+O

CRITICAL READING:
Mastery Test 3

A. 1. C   **B.** 7. C
2. B   8. B
3. D   9. F
4. C   10. A
5. B
6. D

CRITICAL READING:
Mastery Test 4

A. 1. D   **B.** 7. F
2. C   8. C
3. C   9. B
4. A   10. D
5. D
6. B

CRITICAL READING:
Mastery Test 5

A. 1. A   **B.** 6. A
2. B   7. B
3. B   8. C
4. A   9. A
5. C   10. B

CRITICAL READING:
Mastery Test 6

A. 1. C   **B.** 6. C
2. B   7. A
3. C   8. B
4. A   9. A
5. B   10. C

ACTIVE READING AND STUDY:
Review Test 1

1. examples
2. mark
3. write
4. preview
5. recite

ACTIVE READING AND STUDY:
Mastery Test 1
(Wording of answers may vary.)

Definition of phobia:—An intense, unrealistic fear

1. Specific—least disruptive
   Ex.—Fear of heights
2. Social—extreme anxiety about social interactions, especially with strangers and in which the person might be evaluated negatively
   Ex.—Job interview
3. Agoraphobia—most impairing of all phobias; means "fear of open spaces" and involves intense fear of leaving one's home or other familiar places
   Ex.—Individual so totally bound to home that even trip to the mailbox is intolerable

ACTIVE READING AND STUDY:
Mastery Test 3
(Wording of answers may vary.)

Why both men and women drink:
1. Tension relaxation
2. Compensatory drinking—alcohol to heighten sense of masculinity or femininity

One theory why men drink:
Confirmatory drinking—to reinforce the image of masculinity associated with drinking

Other reasons for drinking:
1. Inherited susceptibility. Genetics, especially with females, accounts for 50 to 60 percent of vulnerability to a serious drinking problem.
2. Childhood traumas—especially females abused as children or distressed because of poverty or parental death
3. Depression—especially women and young men
4. Relationship issues. The single, separated, or divorced drink more than the married.
5. Psychological factors—to compensate for feelings of inadequacy
6. Employment—especially women without paying jobs
7. Self-medication—especially women who tell themselves alcohol is a medicine

ACTIVE READING AND STUDY:
Review Test 2

1.	D	6.	C	8. A
2.	A	7.	S	9. B
3.	D		P	10. D
4.	B		S	
5.	D		X	

ACTIVE READING AND STUDY:
Mastery Test 2
(Wording of answers may vary.)

Ex.—Instead of saying "Advertising is the weakest department in the corporation," say "I believe advertising is the weakest department in the corporation."

1. To strengthen the power of their statements.
   Ex.—"Everybody thinks Collins is unfair" has more power than "I think Collins is unfair."
2. To escape responsibility.
   Ex.—It's far more difficult to say "I don't like Herb" than it is to say "No one likes Herb."

ACTIVE READING AND STUDY:
Mastery Test 4
(Wording of answers may vary.)

Who wins congressional elections?
Usually incumbents (individuals who already hold office)—more than 90 percent of them, with 60 percent of the vote.

Why is the picture different in the Senate?
1. Entire state is more diverse than a congressional district, providing a larger base for opposition to an incumbent.
2. Senators have less personal contact with potential voters.
3. Senators receive more coverage in the media and are more likely to be held accountable on controversial issues.
4. Senators tend to draw more visible challengers, whom the voters know and who have more financial backing.

ACTIVE READING AND STUDY:
Final Activity
Sample study notes (wording of student notes may vary):

Impression management—usually conscious efforts by people to influence how others think of them
   Example—In simulated job interviews, women who believed that the interviewer held traditional views of women behaved in a more traditionally feminine way.

Reasons to use impression management:
1. To claim a particular lifestyle
2. To gain approval from others
3. To get a job, date, promotion, etc.

Common self-presentation strategies:
1. Ingratiation—behaving in ways to make oneself likable
   Ex.—giving compliments, doing favors
2. Self-promotion—playing up your strong points
   Ex.—in a job interview, mentioning your school achievements
3. Exemplification—demonstrating behavior worth imitating
   Ex.—behaving consistently according to high ethical standards
4. Intimidation—sending a "don't mess with me" message (usually works only in nonvoluntary relationships)
   Ex.—threats, withholding of something valuable
5. Supplication—presenting oneself as weak and dependent
   Ex.—pleading or crying in an instructor's office

ACTIVE READING AND STUDY:
Mastery Test 5
(Wording of answers may vary.)

The Laws of Thermodynamics—Time-honored principles that describe the behavior of energy.

1. *The First Law*—Energy can neither be created nor destroyed, but it can be converted from one form to another.

> *Ex.*—In a lawnmower, chemical energy converts to heat energy and then to mechanical energy (energy of motion).

2. *The Second Law*—Energy transitions are imperfect—some energy is always lost, usually as heat, in each transition.

> *Ex.*—In the transition from chemical bond energy in gasoline to mechanical energy in a spinning lawnmower blade, much of the original energy is lost as heat, which is normally not available to do useful work.

ACTIVE READING AND STUDY:
Mastery Test 6
(Wording of answers may vary.)

Central point:
One researcher (Herzberg) has provided a list of motivational factors, or satisfiers, that can be said to motivate individuals and produce job satisfaction.

1. Achievement—feeling that you've accomplished a goal (something that you've started).

2. Recognition—provides a feeling of worth and self-esteem.

3. The job itself—people who like their jobs tend to be far more motivated to avoid absenteeism and lateness.

4. Growth and advancement possibilities also motivate people—these are like the old carrot and stick philosophy.

5. Responsibility—provides a sense of accomplishment and fills an internal need to see things done right.

6. Feedback—ideal form is inherent to the job.

> *Ex.*—Radiographer knows right away if an x-ray film she has taken is good.

Answers to the Reading Selections in Part II

1 PERSONAL CONFLICT STYLES

Reading Comprehension Questions

1. D	6. A	11. A	16. B
2. B	7. C	12. B	17. D
3. D	8. D	13. A	18. B
4. A	9. D	14. A	19. C
5. C	10. C	15. D	20. B

Study Notes *(Note: Wording of answers may vary.)*

Central point: People respond in different ways when faced with a conflict situation.

1. Nonassertive behavior—the inability or unwillingness to express thoughts or feelings in a conflict

A surprisingly common way of dealing with conflicts
Takes different forms:
a. Avoidance—either physical (avoiding a friend after an argument) or conversational (changing the topic)
    b. Accommodation—putting others' needs ahead of own
    Ex.—Close window and turn up radio to deal with barking dog.

2. Direct aggression—a criticism or demand that threatens the face of the person at whom it is directed
Includes character and physical appearance attacks
    Ex.—Could respond to barking dog by abusively confronting your neighbor
Can severely punish attacker and victim

3. Passive aggression—expressing hostility in an obscure or manipulative way—"crazymaking"
    Ex.—Complain anonymously to the city pound and then express sympathy after dog hauled away.

4. Indirect communication—convey a message in a roundabout manner in order to save face for the recipient
    Ex.—Strike up a friendly conversation with dog owners and ask if anything you're doing is too noisy for them.

5. Assertion—expressing the speaker's needs, thoughts, and feelings clearly and directly without judging or dictating to others
    Ex.—Explain your problem about the dog to your neighbor to see if you can work together to find a solution.

2 CARDIOVASCULAR DISEASE RISK FACTORS

Reading Comprehension Questions

1. D	6. B	11. A	16. S, S, X, P
2. C	7. C	12. D	17. A
3. C	8. B	13. A	18. B
4. A	9. B	14. C	19. C
5. D	10. C	15. B	20. B

Study Notes *(Note: Wording of answers may vary.)*

Central point: To prevent heart disease, everyone should learn about the ten cardiovascular risk factors and eliminate as many of them as possible.

1. Risk Factors That Cannot Be Changed:
    a. Increasing Age—*nearly 84% of people who die from heart disease are aged 65 or over.*
    b. *Male Gender—men have greater risk of heart disease than do women prior to age 55.*
    c. Heredity—*children may have genetic predisposition (tendency) to develop heart disease. Race is also a related consideration; prevalence of hypertension among African Americans is among the highest in the U.S.*

2. Risk Factors That Can Be Changed:
    a. Tobacco Smoke—*About 46.5 million adults and about 28.5% of high school students smoke. Smokers have a heart attack risk more than twice that of nonsmokers.*
    Heart attack risk is about 30% greater for people exposed to secondhand smoke in the home.
    Good news—heart attack risk declines rapidly when a person stops smoking.
    b. Physical Inactivity—*Regular aerobic exercise strengthens heart muscle, lowers blood cholesterol, moderates stress, and more.*
    60% of Americans are not physically active enough.
    Sustained, vigorous physical activity produces strong reduction in CVD.
    c. High Blood Cholesterol Level—*About 102 million American adults have a total cholesterol level of greater than 200 mg/dl.*
    The higher the level, the greater the risk for heart disease.
    Drugs and diet can control.
    d. *High Blood Pressure*—About 58 million Americans have hypertension, which can seriously damage a person's heart and blood vessels. It can be controlled.
    e. *Diabetes Mellitus*—A debilitating chronic disease; over 17 million Americans have diabetes, which can cause heart and blood vessel damage. It can be controlled.
    f. *Obesity and Overweight—Over 60 % of American adults are overweight, and 26% are obese. More likely to develop heart disease and stroke.*

3. *Another Risk Factor Contributing to Heart Disease:*
Unresolved stress over a long period can contribute to heart disease.

3 COLLECTIVE BEHAVIOR

Reading Comprehension Questions

1. C	6. D	11. B	16. P, S, X, S
2. C	7. D	12. C	17. A
3. B	8. B	13. B	18. A
4. A	9. A	14. B	19. B
5. C	10. C	15. S,P,S,X	20. C

Study Notes *(Note: Wording of answers may vary.)*

Central point: Collective behaviors—ways of thinking, feeling, and acting that develop among a large number of people and that are relatively spontaneous and unstructured

Varieties of Collective Behavior:

1. Rumors—A rumor is a difficult-to-verify piece of information transmitted from person to person in relatively rapid fashion.

> *Ex.—After the 9-11-01 terrorist attacks, rumors flew about biological and chemical weapon attacks. On Internet, rumors spread very quickly.*

2. Fashions and Fads

Fashion—a folkway that lasts for a short time and enjoys widespread acceptance within society

> *Ex.—Black dresses are "in" for women one year; jeans another.*

Fad—a folkway that lasts for a short time and enjoys acceptance among only a segment of the population

> *Ex.—Dance or song*

Adolescents prone to fads; provide a sense of identity and are signs of in-group and out-group status.

> *Craze—a fad that is an all-consuming passion*
> *Ex.—Famous tulip mania in Holland in 17th century*

3. Mass hysteria—refers to the rapid dissemination of behaviors involving contagious anxiety, usually associated with some mysterious force.

> *Ex.—Medieval witch hunts rested on belief that social ills were caused by witches.*

Mass psychogenic illness—"epidemics" of assembly-line illness: workers making dresses, for example, complain of nausea, etc.

Usually a collective response to severe stress

4. Panic—involves irrational and uncoordinated but collective actions among people induced by the presence of an immediate, severe threat.

> *Ex.—People commonly flee from a catastrophe such as flood.*
> *Another ex.—SARS epidemic in China became an information epidemic causing panic about the disease.*

5. Crowds—temporary, relatively unorganized gatherings of people in close physical proximity

Four basic types of crowds:

a. Casual crowd—a collection of people who have little in common except that they may be viewing a common event, such as a movie

b. Conventional crowd—a number of people who have assembled for some specific purpose and who typically act in accordance with established norms, such as people attending a baseball game or a concert

c. Expressive crowd—an aggregation of people who have gotten together for self-stimulation and personal gratification, such as occurs at a religious revival or a rock festival

d. Acting crowd—an excited, volatile collection of people engaged in rioting, looting, or other forms of aggressive behavior in which established norms carry little weight

Shared characteristics of crowds:

1. Suggestibility—susceptible to directions, etc.

2. Deindividuation—people are less inhibited in committing disapproved acts in a group.

3. Invulnerability—people acquire a sense they are powerful and invincible and may, for example, steal or vandalize as a result.

4 TYPES OF NONVERBAL SYMBOLS

Reading Comprehension Questions

1. D	6. A	11. D	16. B
2. D	7. A	12. D	17. A
3. C	8. B	13. B	18. C
4. D	9. C	14. C	19. S, P, S, X
5. A	10. B	15. B	20. A

Study Notes *(Note: Wording of answers may vary.)*

Central point: We communicate nonverbally in a number of ways.

1. The Eyes

—Single most important area for nonverbal communication; people pay attention not only to eye expressions but also to amount of eye contact.

—Eye contact conveys message of warmth and concern for the listener and trust and sincerity in business situations.

— Beware of giving too much eye contact (as to boss or member of opposite sex or someone on the street); it may seem impolite or threatening.

2. The Face and Head

—The eyebrows along with eyes are one of most expressive areas of the face. Quickly raising both eyebrows is a way to acknowledge someone.

—The mouth is highly expressive, with the most well known nonverbal clue being the smile. Tightening the mouth can mean anger; biting one side can mean fear; opening it can mean surprise.

— The most common head movements are nodding and shaking the head to say "Yes" and "No." Use the nod selectively. Many other messages in head movements.

> *Ex.—turning the head away can mean the end of a communication.*

3. Gestures

—Hand gestures are almost as expressive as facial gestures. Most common hand gesture is waving hello or goodbye.

—Many hand and arm gestures. Ex.—crossing arms in front of chest expresses a closed attitude.

— Handshake should be firm with elbow pumped about three to six times.

4. Touch

—Strict rules govern acceptable ways to touch in an organization. Touch in general is seen as a sign of caring and concern. In business it is generally acceptable when it is to the upper back or to the arm.

— A touch that lasts too long can have sexual overtones. Another relationship that governs touch is rank, with people of higher rank able to initiate touch with those of lower rank.

5 SPORTS: ILLUSTRATING THE THREE PERSPECTIVES

Reading Comprehension Questions

1. D	6. B	11. B	16. C
2. A	7. B	12. D	17. B
3. C	8. D	13. C	18. C
4. C	9. B	14. A	19. A
5. D	10. C	15. S,S,P,S	20. C

Study Notes *(Note: Wording of answers may vary.)*

Central point: *Three sociological perspectives can help us understand the significance of sports in our lives.*

1. Sports as Beneficial to Society
— *Functionalist perspective: Society consists of interdependent groups cooperating to pursue common goals.*
— *According to this perspective, sports perform three major functions:*
    a. Conducive to success in other areas of life.
      Ex.—athletes or spectators learn the importance of hard work, playing by the rules, and teamwork.
    b. Enhance health and happiness.
      Ex.—physical and emotional benefits for runners. Improved quality of life for spectators.
    c. Contribute to social order and stability by serving as an integrating force for society as a whole.
      Can bring together people of diverse racial, social, and cultural backgrounds.

2. Sports as Harmful to Society
—*Conflict perspective: Society is made up of conflicting groups, such as men and women, each pursuing their own interests.*
— *According to this perspective, sports harm society by serving the interests of the powerful over the powerless in two ways:*
    a. Act as an opiate, numbing the masses' sense of dissatisfaction with capitalist society.
      Ex.—involvement in sports as spectators distracts low-paid workers from their undesirable jobs.
    b. Reinforce social, gender, and racial inequalities in society.
      Ex.—people have turned into "couch potatoes" who spend more time watching than playing sports. Sports are big business for benefit of a tiny group of owners and players who become tycoons and superstars.
— *Women's programs have expanded, but sports are still a "man's world."*
— *A few African Americans have benefited, but most sports offer a false hope that perpetuates the high rate of poverty among blacks.*

3. Sports as Symbolic Interaction
—*Symbolic interactionist perspective: Society is composed of individuals interpreting each other's behavior and constantly negotiating with each other.*
— *According to this perspective, sports help us understand how we behave.*
    Ex.—Coaches instill the idea of winning into their players. Players see themselves as winners, so they win.
    Ex.—Coaches see African Americans as superior athletes (stereotyping), so they expect more of these athletes, who then outperform white teammates. Stereotyping also discourages women from participating in "male" sports.

6 A CIVIL WAR SOLDIER'S LETTER TO HIS WIFE

Reading Comprehension Questions

1. B	6. B	11. C	16. A
2. B	7. D	12. A	17. D
3. D	8. B	13. D	18. S, S, P, S
4. C	9. C	14. B	19. A
5. C	10. B	15. D	20. B

Summarizing *(Note: Wording of answers may vary.)*

1. lay down nearly all of hers
2. bitter fruit of orphanage
3. irresistibly *or* to the battlefield
4. watch them from the spirit land
5. confidence

7 SINGLE-SEX SCHOOLS

Reading Comprehension Questions

1. C	6. D	11. B	16. C
2. C	7. C	12. D	17. S, P, S, X
3. A	8. B	13. D	18. A
4. B	9. A	14. C	19. B
5. B	10. D	15. A	20. C

Outlining *(Note: Wording of answers may vary.)*

1c. Girls could be introduced to math and science concepts in ways that particularly appeal to them.
2a. Flirting takes up a lot of time and energy that could be better used in the classroom.
3a. Girls wouldn't have to make a point of being clueless in math.
3d. Boys would not feel compelled to be "jocks," noisy, disruptive, and overbearing.

8 A KING'S FOLLY

Reading Comprehension Questions

1. C	6. C	11. B	16. A
2. B	7. D	12. D	17. C
3. D	8. D	13. D	18. C
4. B	9. D	14. D	19. B
5. C	10. B	15. D	20. B

Summarizing *(Note: Wording of answers may vary.)*

1. how much his daughters claim to love him
2. as a daughter should
3. leave her castle and go to stay with Regan
4. judgment and vision
5. finds the king and persuades him to take shelter
6. tie him to a chair
7. feel love and desire for Edmund
8. he has ordered the deaths of the king and Cordelia
9. the dead Cordelia
10. becomes the ruler

9 IN MY DAY

Reading Comprehension Questions

1. A	6. C	11. B	16. D
2. B	7. B	12. D	17. D
3. C	8. C	13. A	18. D
4. D	9. D	14. B	19. A
5. A	10. A	15. C	20. D

Summarizing *(Note: Wording of answers may vary.)*

1. failing to recognize him

2. calling him on the phone to tell him that she is being buried that day

3. break free from a lonely and boring old age and to return mentally to a time when she was loved and needed

4. give her a pep talk to boost her spirits

5. parents, like other people, can "become frail and break"

6. knows very little about his mother's childhood and her people

7. lectures them about the hardships he endured growing up

8. selective and therefore dishonest

9. was still able to answer his questions

10. break free from their parents and create their own pasts

10 THE SPIDER AND THE WASP

Reading Comprehension Questions

1. B	6. B	11. C	16. C
2. A	7. D	12. C	17. C
3. D	8. A	13. A	18. A
4. D	9. C	14. A	19. B
5. C	10. A	15. B	20. C

Outlining *(Note: Wording of answers may vary.)*

1. Before the attack

1c. After the wasp is satisfied that the tarantula is the correct species, she digs the spider's grave.

2b. She corners the tarantula and grasps one of its legs in her jaws.

3b. The wasp drags the tarantula down to the bottom of the grave.

Answers to the Combined-Skills Tests in Part III

COMBINED SKILLS: Test 1
1. B   5. A
2. C   6. B
3. C   7. C
4. D   8. C

COMBINED SKILLS: Test 2
1. B   5. A
2. C   6. B
3. D   7. A
4. B   8. A

COMBINED SKILLS: Test 3
1. D   5. B
2. B   6. B
3. B   7. D
4. C   8. A

COMBINED SKILLS: Test 4
1. B   5. D
2. C   6. D
3. T   7. B
4. A   8. C

COMBINED SKILLS: Test 5
1. B   5. D
2. D   6. B
3. D   7. B
4. C   8. D

COMBINED SKILLS: Test 6
1. B   5. A
2. C   6. B
3. B   7. C
4. A   8. B

COMBINED SKILLS: Test 7
1. A   5. A
2. C   6. C
3. B   7. D
4. C   8. C

COMBINED SKILLS: Test 8
1. B   5. C
2. D   6. A
3. T   7. A
4. B   8. A

COMBINED SKILLS: Test 9
1. D   5. D
2. C   6. D
3. A   7. B
4. C   8. C

COMBINED SKILLS: Test 10
1. B   5. B
2. C   6. C
3. A   7. B
4. D   8. A

COMBINED SKILLS: Test 11
1. B   5. D
2. C   6. D
3. B   7. A
4. D   8. A

COMBINED SKILLS: Test 12
1. B   5. A
2. D   6. D
3. B   7. C
4. D   8. C

COMBINED SKILLS: Test 13
1. B   5. A
2. D   6. D
3. D   7. A
4. B   8. C

COMBINED SKILLS: Test 14
1. C   5. D
2. C   6. D
3. B   7. B
4. C   8. D

COMBINED SKILLS: Test 15
1. B   5. B
2. B   6. A
3. A   7. A
4. D   8. B

COMBINED SKILLS: Test 16
1. D   5. A
2. C   6. B
3. D   7. A
4. A   8. D

COMBINED SKILLS: Test 17
1. C   5. A
2. C   6. A
3. A   7. D
4. A   8. D

COMBINED SKILLS: Test 18
1. D   5. D
2. C   6. A
3. C   7. A
4. C   8. D

COMBINED SKILLS: Test 19
1. C   5. C
2. D   6. D
3. D   7. A
4. A   8. B

COMBINED SKILLS: Test 20
1. D   5. A
2. C   6. B
3. C   7. B
4. C   8. A

SUGGESTED ANSWERS TO THE DISCUSSION QUESTIONS IN PART I

Note: For some questions, additional related questions have been included to enhance class discussion.

1 Getting a Good Night's Sleep

1. *How much sleep do you typically get in a night? Do you feel that you sleep enough? If not, what do you think are the major reasons you aren't sleeping more? What are some ways in which you could restructure your life in order to get a full eight hours of sleep a night?*

   Answers will vary.

2. *A scientist quoted in paragraph 1 compares sleep with food, but notes that while we would not accept being deprived of food, we accept being sleep-deprived. Why do you think so many people simply accept the fact that they don't get enough sleep?*

   Some possible answers: In our hectic society, being sleep-deprived is regarded as normal. Many people's schedules are overly full—by necessity or by choice—and they see skimping on sleep as the only way to get by. Also, getting enough sleep takes planning and prioritizing. If one is a fan of late-night television, for instance, it takes discipline to give up TV-watching in favor of sleep. In addition, being able to "get by" on little sleep is somehow regarded as an admirable thing. People who need plenty of sleep may be regarded as lazy or self-indulgent.

3. *The selection mentions nodding off at meetings and falling asleep at the wheel as two potential consequences of sleep deprivation. What are some other negative consequences that you can think of? Conversely, what might some positive consequences be if people got more sleep?*

   Possible negative consequences of sleep deprivation include doing a sloppy job at work, becoming short-tempered, having trouble focusing one's attention, depression, memory lapses. Positive consequences of adequate sleep include more energy, sharper intellect, more attractive appearance (bright eyes, better color, etc.), better mood, and generally better physical health.

4. *In your view, are there any factors which contribute to Americans' sleep deprivation other than those mentioned in the selection? If so, what are they, and what—if anything—could be done to counteract them?*

   Answers will vary.

2 Drug-Altered Consciousness

1. Were you surprised by some of the facts mentioned in this reading? If so, what surprised you?

Answers will vary.

2. Why do you think people are drawn to the use of mood-altering substances? Are drug- and alcohol-users necessarily unhappy with the reality of their lives? Why might they want to change their mood?

While some drug and alcohol users are clearly trying to escape unhappy realities in their lives, many more are not (although continued drug and alcohol use can cause unhappiness, thus setting up a cycle of abuse). Many people use drugs or alcohol simply because they enjoy the effects—the temporary loss of inhibitions, the brief euphoria. Perhaps they are bored, or shy in social situations, or wanting to fit in with friends who are using drugs or alcohol. Perhaps they think they can be more relaxed, funnier, or more successful romantically if they are drunk or high.

3. From this reading, we can infer that for centuries, the use of mood-altering substances was regarded as morally neutral, sometimes even positive. The reading suggests that it is only in relatively recent times that such substance use has been looked at with disapproval. Why do you think these attitudes have changed?

Here are two possible reasons:
- As indicated in the article, the use of drugs and alcohol traditionally took place in a community setting—as part of a religious service, for instance. Community controls were in place to keep an individual from acting in disapproved-upon fashion.
- The use of drugs and alcohol is linked to violence, injury, and death more now than in the past. In past centuries, drug-impaired people did not get behind the wheel of an automobile. With the rise of extremely addictive drugs like crack cocaine, people are far more likely to resort to crime to obtain drugs than they were in the past.

4. In contrast to other times and cultures, Americans tend to use drugs that they know to be harmful. In your opinion, what are some of the major causes of drug and alcohol abuse in our country?

Possible answers:
- Movies, ads, books, music videos, etc., often portray drug and alcohol use as hip, glamorous, and fun.
- Unemployment, the threat of terrorism, global warming, war, and other highly stressful influences make people feel powerless and uncertain of the future. Rather than think about such difficult topics, they may choose to get high.

3 "Extra Large," Please

1. When you were a child, how much—and what kinds of—exercise did you typically get? Did you grow up in a place where kids could and did play outside? If not, were you able—or encouraged—to find opportunities to exercise?

Answers will vary.

2. *The author of the selection proposes that fast-food restaurants should be required to display clear nutritional information about their products. Do you think that the presentation of this information would result in a significant reduction in the amount of fast food that people consume? Would it change your eating habits? Why or why not?*

Answers will vary.

3. *Recently, some people have attempted to sue fast-food companies, claiming that consuming their food has led to a host of serious health problems. What is your opinion of these lawsuits? Should fast-food manufacturers and advertisers be held liable for our society's obesity problem? Or are individuals the only ones responsible for their weight? Explain your reasoning.*

Answers will vary.

4. *The author admits that when she was a kid, she probably would have preferred pizza to something more nutritious. She also mentions that eight out of ten California students failed a basic fitness test. Given the fact that most kids prefer fast foods and passive entertainment, what can be done to promote healthier lifestyles to young people?*

Some possible answers:
- Make physical education a regular part of every child's school day.
- Eliminate junk food from school buildings and cafeterias.
- Limit or ban junk food advertising from TV shows aimed at children.
- Set up more community recreation centers when kids can play together safely.
- Educate parents about the need to limit passive TV and computer time and encourage physical activity.

4 Skills of Effective Face-To-Face Conversationalists

1. *Do you consider yourself a talkative person—or a quiet person? Which of the specific skills mentioned in this essay would be valuable for you to work on? Which of them do you think would work less well for you? Explain.*

Answers will vary.

2. *Think of the last time you had an extremely interesting conversation with someone. What was it about the conversation, or the conversationalist, that made it so interesting?*

Answers will vary.

3. *Have you ever been in a conversation with someone who dominated the conversation? Conversely, have you ever tried to carry on a conversation with a person who failed to provide any "free information," or who demonstrated other inappropriate conversational behaviors? If so, how did you react in each situation?*

Answers will vary.

4. *In your opinion, what advantages do people who are skilled conversationalists have over people who are not?*

Possible answers:

- Skilled conversationalists learn more, because they listen to others as well as talk.

- Skilled conversationalists are generally better liked than unskilled conversationalists. Others appreciate their ability to draw people out.

- Skilled conversationalists are good at getting their point of view across. This gives them an edge in, for example, winning an argument or persuading an interviewer that they are good candidates for a job.

5   Hoover and Hard Times: 1929–1933

1. *This reading provides a great many facts about how the Great Depression affected various parts of the U.S. population. What did you learn from the reading that surprised you most?*

Answers will vary.

2. *The selection mentions that African Americans and people of Mexican origin were particularly hard hit during the depression, often facing discrimination as the competition for jobs became desperate. In your opinion, has the position of African Americans and Latinos improved since the depression, worsened, or stayed about the same? Explain your reasoning.*

Answers will vary.

3. *The authors spend most of their time describing the economic impact of the depression. In the final paragraph, however, they mention "the psychological impact of the depression." From what you have read here, what psychological effects would you infer the depression had on various groups?*

It is reasonable to conclude that during the economic depression, many people suffered from psychological depression, sadness, and feelings of despair. Parents must have felt a great sense of failure that they could not support their children. Husbands and fathers must have been devastated that they could not fill their traditional role as providers. African American and Mexican American workers must have been enraged to see their jobs, formerly scorned by white people, taken away so that whites could have them.

4. *The Great Depression led to economic hardship and social upheaval, yet somehow our system of government remained stable. How do you think Americans would respond today if we experienced a depression? For instance, how might the government respond if the unemployment rate reached 25 percent? How might the American public respond to widespread unemployment and reduction in wages?*

Answers will vary.

6 The Ugly Truth About Beauty

1. *Although Barry's piece is written for laughs, he obviously has something serious to say about women and men and their feelings about their appearances. In non-humorous language, how would you rephrase his main points?*

   Possible answers:
   • Women are chronically dissatisfied with their looks.

   • Men are much less worried about their looks than women are.

   • Barbie dolls and other cultural influences create an impossible physical standard for women.

   • Men do not notice a lot of what women do to themselves to be beautiful.

2. *Think about the women you know. How much time would you say that they devote to clothing, hairstyles, and makeup? On the basis of your answer, do you agree with the author's view that women spend far too much time worrying about how they look? Why or why not?*

   Answers will vary.

3. *Do you agree or disagree with the author's negative view of the role Barbie dolls play in shaping American girls' image of themselves? Once the girls have grown up, to what extent would you say that external forces, such as the media and the fashion industry, influence their feelings about their own appearances? Explain your reasoning.*

   Answers will vary, but it is hard to imagine that the endless stream of media stories—such as women's magazines crammed with stories about weight loss, makeup, hairstyles, plastic surgery, etc.,—do *not* influence many women to think that they are not "good enough."

4. *Do you agree with Barry that men are generally satisfied with their own appearance? Why might their standards be so different from those of women?*

   Answers to the first question will vary. Possible answers to the second question include the idea that men have traditionally had their value measured not by their physical appearance, but by their accomplishments and their ability to be good providers.

7 White-Collar Crime

1. *The article mentions that none of the Ford executives who were responsible for the Pinto-related deaths were ever arrested and that, in fact, they remained respected members of their communities. Why do you think this happened? What factors might have led them to escape punishment and public censure?*

   Possible answers: The Ford executives didn't fit the stereotypes that many people hold of criminals. They were, in all likelihood, upper-middle-class, well-spoken, well-dressed white men. They were probably socially prominent in their communities, very likely supporters of local charities, etc. And even though they made business decisions that led to the deaths of the Pinto victims, they did not directly kill them—they did not personally shoot or stab them to death. Their distance from the actual killing probably made it easier for their community members to think they were not really guilty of anything too bad.

2. *If white-collar crime takes a greater economic toll than street crime, why do you think most people are so much more indignant and angry about street crime?*

Ordinary people see the consequences of street crime with their own eyes. Street crimes, such as mugging, murder, rape, and carjacking, are easy to comprehend and to feel angry about. We can all imagine ourselves as being victims of street crime. By contrast, white-collar crime is more complex, harder to understand. Most people do not worry often about being victims of white-collar crime.

3. *Do you agree that "The powerful can and do manipulate our legal system. They can and do escape punishment for their crimes"? Can you think of other examples that demonstrate this point?*

Answers will vary.

4. *What, if anything, can society do to ensure that white-collar criminals do not escape punishment for the crimes they commit?*

Answers will vary.

8 A Vote Against Legalizing Drugs

1. *Before reading this essay, did you agree that drugs should be legalized—or did you disagree? Did the essay change your opinion in any way? If so, which of the author's points did you find most convincing?*

Answers will vary.

2. *Do you think drug abuse prevention programs, of the sort offered in many elementary and middle schools, are effective? Why or why not? What could make them work better?*

Answers will vary.

3. *The author states that the underprivileged turn to drugs as an escape from their wretched lives. Yet drug abuse is a growing problem in middle-class and wealthy communities as well. Why do you think this is so?*

Middle-class people may think of drugs as being recreational rather than "an escape from their wretched lives." Also, middle-class and wealthy people have their own sources of stress. Job problems, "keeping up with the Joneses," trying to maintain an image of success, and overwork could all lead to drug abuse.

4. *Imagine that you have just been elected president of the United States after promising the voters that you will do something significant to address the nation's drug problem. What steps would you take?*

Answers will vary.

9 A Scary Time to Raise a Daughter

1. *Do you agree with Lopez that this is a particularly challenging time to raise a child? Which of his concerns do you share? Do you think his concerns are groundless or exaggerated?*

Answers will vary.

2. *How much effect do you believe that marketing campaigns such as Abercrombie & Fitch's have on young people and their views on sexuality? Do you agree with the author that such messages result in negative consequences for young people, especially girls—or do you disagree? Explain.*

Answers will vary.

3. *According to the selection, 50% of rape victims are 18 or younger, and the rapists are acquaintances 80% of the time. In your view, what changes can we make as a society to help ensure that fewer girls and young women fall victim to rape?*

Answers will vary, but students might suggest some of the following:
- Educate girls that they are not obligated to be "nice" to people who are trying to take advantage of them. Not infrequently, girls are so concerned about not hurting someone's feelings that they are reluctant to speak up for themselves strongly and forcefully.
- Educate boys that "date rape" is as morally and legally wrong as any other kind of rape. Parents should make sure their sons understand that girls do not "owe" anyone sex.

4. *Why do you think Lopez is particularly concerned about raising a girl in today's society? How is the impact of a sexualized society different for boys than it is for girls?*

In our society, boys often receive the message that they should focus on "scoring," getting as many sexual partners as possible. Girls, then, may become viewed as potential sexual partners rather than as individuals. Lopez worries about his daughter being targeted in such a way.

10 Impression Management

1. *Discuss a time when you (or someone you know) used one of the strategies mentioned in the selection to make an impression. What happened as a result? On the basis of this result, would you say the strategy worked? Why or why not?*

Answers will vary.

2. *In the second paragraph of the reading, the example is given of how job applicants might alter their behavior in response to what they believed to be true about the interviewer. To what extent do you think this alteration in behavior is a good strategy when job-seeking? What could be its downside?*

Answers to the first question will vary. The downside of such behavior is that job-seekers risk being hired under false pretenses, as it were. If the woman described in the essay is hired partially because she is "traditionally feminine," it may create problems later if she does not continue to present herself that way.

3. *The authors point out that choices in such things as dress, hairstyle, and manner of speech act as a sort of shorthand by which a person declares "I am a member of this group." What are some of the particular "identities" that you see people currently declaring in their fashion and language choices? What groups are they claiming membership in?*

Answers will vary.

4. *In your view, in which occupations is it particularly important to make a good impression? Why?*

Answers will vary.

SUGGESTED ANSWERS TO THE DISCUSSION QUESTIONS IN PART II

1 Personal Conflict Styles

1. *How would you have handled the barking dog situation? In general, what would you say is your primary style of behavior in a conflict situation?*

   In answering, students can categorize themselves as nonassertive, directly aggressive, passive-aggressive, indirect, or assertive. Do they ignore unpleasant situations? Act aggressively demanding? Send aggressive messages in indirect, "crazymaking" ways? Drop indirect hints? Or clearly express their needs?

2. *The authors state: "Over a five-day period, spouses reported that their partner engaged in an average of thirteen behaviors that were 'displeasurable' to them but that they had only one confrontation during the same period." Do you believe in the policy of letting most "displeasurable behaviors" go by without mentioning them? Or do you think it is better to immediately let a partner, family member, or colleague know when you are displeased about something? Explain your answer.*

   Answers will vary, but students may argue one of two basic positions: (1) That partners cannot be expected to know when you're displeased (and thus change their behavior) unless you tell them, or that (2) a successful relationship requires letting petty "displeasures" slide and confronting the partner only on important issues.

3. *After reading this selection, do you feel that you might try to change your style of behavior in a conflict situation? If so, what style of behavior might you try now, and why?*

   Answers will vary.

4. *It seems that every day we hear stories about people who resort to violence in response to conflict situations. Indeed, the United States has one of the highest murder rates in the world. In your view, why do so many Americans resort to an aggressive style of behavior in responding to conflicts?*

   Answers will vary, but students may suggest a number of theories about why America is such a violent society. The theories may include the following: Guns are easily available. Movies, TV shows, and video games turn violence into entertainment. Class, race, and economic divisions make many American feel angry and powerless, which leads to their lashing out in violent ways.

2 Cardiovascular Disease

1. *Would you say that your risk of developing heart disease is low, medium, or high? Which of the cardiovascular risk factors mentioned in the selection do you possess? On the basis of what you have learned in this reading, is there anything you can do to decrease your risk of developing heart disease? Explain.*

   Answers will vary.

2. *The selection lists the benefits that come with physical activity but states that health professionals are amazed that so many Americans refuse to become regularly active. In your view, why don't more Americans get the recommended amount of physical activity?*

The most common reason that people do not exercise is that it is simply easier not to. Becoming physically active, like any other lifestyle change, requires a decision and follow-through. Remaining in "couch potato" mode is easier. In addition, people often claim they don't have time to exercise, although most of them find time for other, less beneficial activities. Another reason is that they think of exercise as boring and pointless, although they could choose another form of exercise (team sports, dancing, swimming, boxing) that they might enjoy.

3. *The selection mentions that people who are under stress are more likely to develop negative dependence behaviors—for example, smoking, under-activity, poor dietary practices—to deal with the stress. What are some positive ways that you know of that people use to cope with stress? Have you tried any of them? If so, have you found them to be effective? Why or why not?*

Answers will vary, but many people find relief from stress through physical exercise, journaling, meditation, and eating a well-balanced diet. Things as simple as talking with a friend, taking a few deep breaths, taking a hot bath, losing yourself in a good book, or listening to relaxing music can be powerful stress-relievers as well.

4. *The selection states that the best time to start protecting and improving one's cardiovascular system is early in life. We can't go back in time, but we can help to influence the younger generation. How can we encourage the younger generation to develop heart-healthy habits? What negative influences must we overcome to do so?*

We can encourage the young people in our lives to spend less time watching TV, playing video games, or other sedentary activities, and more time engaging in physical activity. We can provide wholesome food and snacks in our homes and discourage the consumption of high-fat, high-sodium snacks, fast foods, and soda. We can talk with our children about the ads they see on TV and elsewhere for unhealthy foods and help them become more critical of the poor nutritional messages they are being given. Rather than do these things in a way that makes kids feel deprived, we can help them feel empowered as people who make positive choices in order to become strong and healthy.

3   Collective Behavior

1. *We have all heard rumors (or seen them on the Internet) and perhaps have helped spread some. What rumors have you heard that later proved to be untrue? What rumors later turned out to be true? After reading this selection, do you have a better idea of which particular subjects or events are likely to give rise to rumors?*

Answers will vary, but events that inspire fear and uncertainty in people (such as a terrorist attack) are likely to inspire rumors.

2. *Reread the author's definitions of "fashion" and "fads" (paragraphs 7–10). What are some current examples of fashions? Of fads? To what extent would you say your own behavior is influenced by fashions or fads? Explain.*

Answers will vary.

3. *Have you ever been part of a group that became caught up in a panic or an example of mass hysteria? What was the situation? How did people behave? Were you aware of individuals who tried to either calm the situation or increase others' anxiety?*

Answers will vary.

4. *Have you ever personally been involved in some type of crowd behavior? If so, was the experience a positive one—or a negative one? Explain.*

Answers will vary.

4   Types of Nonverbal Symbols

1. *What are some of the ways that you (or people you know) communicate nonverbally? What are the messages that you (or they) tend most often to convey? Have these nonverbal messages ever been misunderstood? Explain.*

Answers will vary.

2. *What different does the author note between men's and women's nonverbal communication? What other differences have you noticed? In your opinion, what factors account for these differences?*

The author notes that the rules of touch differ depending on gender. If a handshake or gesture involving touch between a man and woman is not brief and businesslike, it can suggest sexual interest. Answers to the other questions will vary.

3. *Every culture has its own vocabulary of gestures. The author mentions a few common American gestures, such as indicating "OK!" by making a circle with the thumb and first finger. What are some gestures not mentioned here that you are familiar with, and what do they mean? Are they common to a group of friends, an age group, a nationality, a family, or another kind of group?*

Answers will vary.

4. *Now that you have read this selection, are there any forms of nonverbal communication that you would like to be able to use more effectively? In what ways might you benefit if you improved your command of nonverbal communication?*

Answers will vary, but students may now be more aware of how their current nonverbal communication is interpreted—for instance, if they do (or do not) maintain eye contact with people.

5   Sports: Illustrating the Three Perspectives

1. *As the selection makes clear, the influence of sports in our society reaches far and wide. How have sports influenced your life? Would you say that this influence has been positive, negative, or both? Explain.*

Answers will vary.

2. *In the selection, the author presents examples of how the positive self-image of certain athletes seems to improve their performance. Looking back on your life so far, do you believe that the image you have (or had) of yourself has ever influenced your behavior? Explain.*

Answers will vary. Students may explore the concept that "success breeds success"—that is, that people who present themselves as confident and successful are treated as such by those around them, thereby setting up a cycle of success. The opposite is often true—that people who seem to expect failure are treated as failures by those around them.

3. *Do you agree that gender bias is still a factor in sports? What evidence do you have to support your opinion?*

Answers will vary, but students should note that women's sports receive far less media coverage than men's. College scholarships for women's sports are still less widely available than scholarships for men's sports. On the other hand, with the advent of cable and satellite networks, viewers are more likely to be able to find women's sports on TV than in the past. Many high schools offer more sports options for girls than they did in the past, and the number of high-school girls who participate in athletics continues to climb.

4. *As is mentioned in the reading, African American athletes dominate much of the sports world. The author mentions a potentially negative consequence—that African American youngsters may focus on the unrealistic goal of becoming a sports star. Without discouraging them completely, what might parents, teachers, and community leaders do to encourage these young people to consider other, more realistic options?*

A likely reason that many African American youngsters count on careers as sports stars is that the most successful black people they see and hear about are athletes. To balance this fact, parents, teachers, and community leaders should do all they can to give young people exposure to a wide variety of successful African American adults. If kids have access to African American doctors, lawyers, businesspeople, accountants, mechanics, teachers, nurses, writers, photographers, etc., who can talk to the kids about their careers, the youngsters will form a more realistic view of the career paths available to them. Additionally, it would be valuable if athletes would make themselves available to talk to youngsters about the downside of a sports career—the career-ending injuries; the lack of qualifications to pursue a later, different career; and the pressures of being valued only for one's athletic skill.

6   A Civil War Soldier's Letter to His Wife

1. *What does Sullivan Ballou's letter reveal about his character and principles? Does he deserve to be called a hero? Why or why not?*

Ballou's letter reveals him to be a man who was devoted to his family, to God, and to his country. It is apparent that he would have given up his life for any of those three. Answers to the second and third questions will vary.

2. *Do you agree with Sullivan Ballou's decision to fight for what he believed in, even though it meant risking the happiness and security of his wife and children? Why or why not?*

Answers will vary, but will probably fall into two camps: those who believe that Ballou's ultimate duty was to protect his wife and children (thereby making it wrong to risk their happiness and security), and those who believe that his greatest duty was to defend the security of the country that was his and his family's home.

3. *The letter makes clear that author Sullivan Ballou believed he was carrying out a tradition of sacrifice in the defense of liberty that others had begun during the American Revolution. Do you believe that the recent wars in which America has engaged continue this tradition—or depart from it? Explain.*

Answers will vary, but students might want to comment on America's involvement in World War II, the Korean War, the Vietnam War, and the wars in Iraq.

4. *Under what circumstances, if any, would you be willing to sacrifice your life for a cause?*

Answers will vary.

7 Single-Sex Schools: An Old Idea Whose Time Has Come

1. *Which kind of school did you attend, a single-sex school or a co-ed school? Do your own school experiences reflect the observations made by the author concerning mixed and single-sex classrooms? For example, did you have the impression that boys were "just better" at certain skills, and girls were better at others? What might have given you this impression?*

Answers will vary. Students should consider the possibility that they perceived boys or girls as "just better" at certain skills because of the factors mentioned in the essay, such as girls and boys trying to be more attractive to the opposite sex by playing dumb in certain areas.

2. *Do you agree with the conclusion of the selection—that single-sex schools are preferable to co-ed schools? Why or why not?*

Answers will vary.

3. *In your experience, do teachers treat boys and girls differently in the classroom? Have you seen any examples of the kinds of teacher behavior described in this selection? Explain.*

Answers will vary.

4. *The selection mentions the advantages of single-sex schooling. Can you think of any negative consequences of single-sex schooling? If so, what are they?*

Students may mention the lack of opportunity for boys and girls to socialize. They may say that boys and girls need to learn to interact successfully at some point, and that school is the most natural place for that interaction to occur.

8 A King's Folly

1. *Why do you think Lear sets up such a test for his daughters in order to divide his kingdom?*

It is apparent that Lear has forgotten the difference between genuine love and the flattery that his position as king has earned him. He has, in a sense, become addicted to flattery. Like a junkie, he needs frequent "fixes" of praise, and by setting up the contest involving his daughters, he assumes he will receive an enormous dose of what he desires.

2. *Does the old king deserve what he gets from Regan and Goneril? Why or why not?*

Some students may think that Lear's rejection of his only loving daughter, Cordelia, and his acceptance of his other daughters' obviously empty flattery means that he is a cold, cruel man who deserves what he got. Others may be more sympathetic, saying that Regan and Goneril tricked him and encouraged his bad behavior, and that he was their victim and so deserves pity.

3. *Which character, in your opinion, is the most evil figure in the story? Which character, after Cordelia, most embodies good in humankind?*

Answers will vary, but a case can be made that Regan is the most evil character. She not only abuses her own father, but viciously blinds his old friend, Gloucester. Edmund, who betrays his own father, turns the sisters against one another, and orders the deaths of Cordelia and Lear, is also a good candidate for most evil. Many people would call Kent the most admirable figure in the story, after Cordelia. Without regard for his own safety or status, he criticizes Lear's foolish actions. After Lear exiles him, he loyally stays nearby, watching out for his old friend's welfare.

4. *After they have gotten what they wanted from him, Goneril and Regan both regard their elderly father as a nuisance and treat him with extreme disrespect. Based upon your experience, is a disrespectful attitude toward the elderly common or uncommon in today's society? Explain.*

Answers will vary.

9 In My Day

1. *How would you describe the author's mother, first as a young woman and then as an elderly one? Do you see any similarities between the young Mrs. Baker and the eighty-year-old Mrs. Baker? Between the eighty-year-old Mrs. Baker and her son Russell?*

As a young woman, Mrs. Baker seems to have been energetic, strong-willed, and opinionated. She was apparently not especially concerned with whether people liked her. As an elderly woman, she has lost physical strength, but is still a sharp-tongued woman with strong opinions. The young and elderly Mrs. Baker are very much the same person, although the elderly Mrs. Baker is lonelier and less content with her life. At the end of the essay, Russell Baker reveals some similarities to his mother as he describes how he delivered opinionated lectures to his sons.

2. *When her mind began to wander, Baker at first tried to bring his mother back to the present. Later, however, he played along with her "trips through time." Do you think he was right to stop correcting her mistakes? Why or why not?*

It is likely that when Mrs. Baker's mind first began to wander, Russell believed she was only momentarily confused and that if he corrected her, he could "fix" her. As it became more apparent that Mrs. Baker's mind was permanently affected, Russell realized she would be more happy and relaxed if he encouraged her "trips through time."

3. *Baker writes that "one thinks of parents differently from other people. Other people can become frail and break, but not parents." Why do you think people hold their parents to higher standards than they do other people, and find it harder to forgive their parents when they fall short?*

Parents are the first and most powerful authority figures in our lives. When we are little, we think of them as almost superhuman figures—bigger, stronger, and smarter than anyone else in our world. We believe they can do anything. Even when we are old enough to know better, it is hard to completely get over our sense that if they try hard enough, parents can be perfect.

4. *Baker now regrets not knowing more of his family history. Once he became curious about his mother's past, she was no longer able to tell him about it. What can you—and other parents and children—do to overcome the "disconnections" between generations so that the family's past history can be preserved for the future?*

There are many ways to preserve your family's history. A few ideas:

- Gather together scattered family photographs and have your older family members help identify the people shown. Label the photographs so you'll have a record of who is who.

- Ask older relatives to write brief accounts of experiences in their lives. For instance, you might ask a grandfather to write about his military service, or an aunt to write about her memories of her parents.

- Interview elderly relatives while their memories are still sharp. Ask them for details about your family tree.

10 The Spider and The Wasp

1. *Many people are frightened or disgusted by spiders and wasps. Yet this writer obviously finds both to be beautiful and fascinating creatures. What details about the wasp and the tarantula surprised or interested you most? What similarities to humans do these two species possess? Finally, what conclusions, if any, can we draw about human behavior on the basis of the interactions between the "intelligent" digger wasps and the "instinctual" tarantulas?*

Answers to the first question will vary. A few similarities between these creatures and humans: The female wasp goes to a lot of trouble to provide food for its young. The tarantula rarely bites unless it is being threatened. Conclusions about human behavior: Students may discuss the question of whether human behavior is dictated more by "intelligence" or by "instinct." Is the "intelligent" wasp operating according to free will? Is it making actual decisions about its behavior? Or is it in its way just as "programmed" as the apparently less intelligent spider?

2. *To us, the behavior of the tarantula with the digger wasp seems suicidal. Yet common sense tells us that the tarantula does not want to die in order to provide food for the wasp's offspring. What alternative explanations might there be for the tarantula's behavior?*

The author suggests that the tarantula is so programmed to not start a fight that it is literally incapable of overcoming that programming, even when its life is at stake. It is only at the very end of the wasp's preparations, when the wasp grabs the tarantula, that the tarantula is "triggered" to begin fighting.

3. *Books, articles, and television shows about animal behavior are often very popular, with adults as well as children. How would you explain the fascination that animal behavior holds for people?*

Answers will vary, but many people are intrigued by creatures with whom we share a planet, and with whom we share many common needs and behaviors, and yet who are dramatically different from us in many ways.

4. *The tarantula, as a creature of instinct, can't choose whether to fight or flee, but people can. Think of a time when you were faced with a threatening situation. Did you choose to flee—or to fight? What factors in the situation helped you make your decision?*

Answers will vary.

TEST BANK

This section contains the following:

- A **Test Bank** (pages 37–126) consisting of four additional Mastery Tests for each chapter in Part One of *Ten Steps to Advanced Reading*, as well as four additional Combined-Skills Mastery Tests—44 tests in all;
- An **answer key** (pages 127–130) to the 44 tests in the test bank.

Instructors whose students are using *Ten Steps to Advanced Reading* in class have permission to reproduce any of these tests on a photocopying machine (or a secure website) as often as needed.

MAIN IDEAS: Test A

The main ideas of the following paragraphs appear at different locations. Identify each main idea by filling in its sentence number in the space provided.

____ 1. [1]In the United States, an average of seventy-three people are killed by lightning strikes every year, but there are many things you can do to protect yourself. [2]Indoors, the leading cause of lightning injury is from land-line telephones, since the electrical charge can travel a long distance through telephone wires. [3]So get off the phone, and stay away from major appliances, because metal pipes, electrical wires and dryer vents can all conduct current into the home. [4]Don't take a bath or shower. [5]Water conducts electricity particularly well. [6]Being outdoors is much more dangerous than being indoors. [7]Swimming is a bad idea. [8]You never want to be the tallest object in the area, or directly underneath the tallest object. [9]Don't take shelter under a tall tree, or in a small structure such as those on golf courses or near athletic fields. [10]They will protect against wind and rain but not against lightning. [11]Take precautions even when the storm seems safely far away, as lightning can travel as much as ten miles, and a strike can come out of a clear blue sky. [12]If your hair starts to stand on end in a thunderstorm, this is a bad sign, as it could mean positive charges are rising through you, seeking the negative charge in the air. [13]Move quickly to a safe place!

____ 2. [1]Inevitable as they now seem to us, skyscrapers only became possible in the latter part of the nineteenth century, when steel-frame buildings and electrically powered elevators were developed. [2]Similarly, the sprawling suburbs that we now take for granted would be unthinkable without superhighways or mass public transportation linking cities and suburbs. [3]These, in turn, are dependent on technological innovations such as steel, railroads, electricity, and the private automobile. [4]Finally, paved streets became common in cities only in the twentieth century, and it wasn't until the 1950s and 1960s that clean air acts were passed in the United States to curb exhaust excesses like those that Londoner Charles Dickens described. [5]A given level of technology, then, has much to do with the urban experience.

____ 3. [1]For most people, fairies are tiny, magical beings who don't really exist. [2]Yet one of the most notorious hoaxes of the 20th century centered around photographs that purported to show actual proof of the existence of fairies. [3]These photographs, taken by Elise Wright and Frances Griffiths, two young cousins living in Cottingley, near Bradford, England, depicted the two in various activities with supposed fairies. [4]The first two photographs were taken in 1917 and showed the fairies as small humans with period style haircuts, dressed in filmy gowns, and with large wings on their backs. [5]As strange as it may seem to us, some very prominent people believed the photos and fairies were real, including Sir Arthur Conan Doyle, famed author of the Sherlock Holmes mystery stories. [6]Doyle went so far as to write a book called *The Coming of the Fairies*, about the Cottingley Fairies and his belief in them. [7]It wasn't until 1981 that the cousins confessed that the photos were fake and the fairies nothing more than cut-outs made of paper and cloth.

___ 4. [1]Many people have an image of nineteenth-century mining based on images from history books. [2]Those images are of plucky, independent miners standing in a stream panning for gold. [3]In reality, retrieving minerals from rock was difficult, expensive, and dangerous. [4]A successful mine required a large labor force, industrial tools, and railroad links. [5]Miners worked way below the earth's surface in poorly ventilated tunnels, with no means for removing human or animal waste. [6]Temperatures could reach as high as 120 degrees. [7]Accidents were part of the job, which depended on blasting equipment and industrial machinery. [8]In 1884, a Montana miner drilled into an unexploded dynamite charge and lost his eyes and ears. [9]He received no compensation, for the court decided that the accident "was the result of an unforeseen and unavoidable accident incident to the risk of mining."

___ 5. [1]In 1798, a few naturalists were skeptically probing a specimen delivered to the British Museum in London, looking for signs that a prankster had slyly stitched the bill of an oversized duck onto the pelt of a small furry mammal. [2]They didn't know it, but they were examining the remains of a platypus, a web-footed mammal about half the size of a house cat. [3]Like the other mammals, the duck-billed platypus has mammary glands and hair. [4]However, like birds and reptiles, it has a cloaca, an enlarged duct through which reproductive cells, feces, and excretions from the kidneys pass. [5]It lays shelled eggs, as birds and most reptiles do. [6]Its young hatch pink and unfinished, as embryonic stages too helpless to fend for themselves. [7]Its fleshy bill does appear ducklike, and its broad, flat, furry tail looks like the one on a beaver. [8]With its unusual traits, the platypus invites us to challenge preconceived notions of what constitutes "an animal."

TEN STEPS TO ADVANCED READING

MAIN IDEAS: Test B

The main ideas of the following paragraphs appear at different locations. Identify each main idea by filling in its sentence number in the space provided.

___ 1. ¹The word "suffrage" refers to the right to vote. ²The women's suffrage movement in the United States succeeded with passage of the 19th Amendment to the Constitution in 1920, but not without numerous setbacks and difficulties. ³In New Jersey, women got the right to vote in 1776, but it was taken away in 1807. ⁴Utah territory granted women's suffrage in 1870, but it was lost in the provisions of the same federal law that prohibited polygamy in 1887. ⁵In the 19th century several anti-suffragette groups were founded. ⁶Often backed by conservative men, these groups argued that women had complete freedom in the home, and that the political arena should be left to men. ⁷The women's suffrage movement gained momentum after 1900 as, one by one, many states began granting women the right to vote. ⁸There was still no national suffrage law, however. ⁹In 1913, when five thousand women marched for the cause in Washington, D.C., a crowd of onlookers became derisive and abusive. ¹⁰The police did not intervene, and more than one hundred women were hospitalized for injuries from the resulting chaos. ¹¹Even when women achieved the vote, nay-saying continued. ¹²Warren G. Harding was the first president elected after passage of the 19th Amendment. ¹³When his presidency was rocked by scandals, some blamed women for supporting the candidate who photographed well and was considered handsome.

___ 2. ¹Why do we dream about the things that fill our heads during sleep? ²A naturalistic study of the impact of daytime events on the content of dreams was conducted by researchers shortly after a major earthquake struck the San Francisco area and caused more than $5 billion in damages and killed 62 people. ³The researchers asked students at two universities in the San Francisco area to keep track of the number of upsetting dreams that they had during a three-week period immediately following the earthquake. ⁴As a control group, students at the University of Arizona who had not been near the earthquake did the same thing. ⁵Not surprisingly, the students in the area of the earthquake reported more vivid, upsetting dreams then the students in Arizona. ⁶In addition, 40 percent of the students in the San Francisco area reported at least one dream about earthquakes, compared with 5 percent of the students in Arizona. ⁷Persons exposed to highly stressful events, such as wars, sometimes have nightmarish dreams about them for many years afterwards. ⁸Clearly, events and concerns in our daily lives are among the most common things that we dream about.

___ 3. ¹On a spring morning during rush hour, in a Metro station in Washington, D.C., a young man opened a violin case and took out his instrument. ²He dropped a couple of bills and a handful of change into the open violin case. ³Then he began to play. ⁴During the next 43 minutes, the man played six classical pieces. ⁵In that time, 1,097 people passed by. ⁶Of that number, 27 tossed in some money—a total of $32.17. ⁷Seven people stopped what they were doing and stood to listen, at least for a minute. ⁸All the rest hurried by. ⁹Most appeared not to notice the musician at all. ¹⁰What they did not know was that the violinist was Joshua Bell, one of the best classical violinists to ever live. ¹¹Three nights before his appearance at the Metro station, he had played for a standing-room-only crowd who paid a minimum of $100 a ticket. ¹²He has won Emmy and Grammy awards. ¹³The *Washington Post* newspaper had set up the experiment of having Bell play at the Metro station. ¹⁴The results seemed to show that in order to appreciate beauty, conditions need to be just right. ¹⁵When people are sitting in a concert hall, they are ready to appreciate a great musician. ¹⁶When they are rushing to work, they are not.

___ 4. ¹Every day, millions of Americans use aspartame, an artificial sweetener found in most diet soft drinks as well as table sweeteners, breath mints, and other low-calorie products, in place of sugar in order to lose weight. ²What many people don't realize is that while consuming aspartame may help them cut calories, there is some evidence it may lead to health problems. ³Aspartame contains methanol, which is known to cause headaches, dizziness, nausea, memory loss, eye damage, and sometimes even blindness in humans. ⁴When methanol is digested by the body, it is broken down into formaldehyde, which causes cancer and birth defects. ⁵Scientists who have studied the effects of aspartame on diabetics have shown that the use of aspartame, rather than helping them manage their diabetes by lowering their sugar intake, may make their symptoms worse over time. ⁶There is also scientific evidence that the chemicals in aspartame can alter the way the brain works, resulting in mood disorders such as depression.

___ 5. ¹The short story is a literary form with certain characteristics that define it. ²First of all, it must be fiction. ³That is, the story is something made up by an author and is not intended to be an historical account of events that really occurred or people who really lived. ⁴Nevertheless, most short stories seek to depict a realistic episode in the life of a person, usually as that person encounters a challenge or difficulty of some kind. ⁵Some attention is paid to describing the setting where the action takes place, and to giving the main character a number of different traits to make him or her seem more believable. ⁶If the short story has an obvious moral or lesson, it may also be called a fable or parable. ⁷The Irish writer James Joyce borrowed the religious term "epiphany" to describe a moment of realization or new understanding that often occurs at the climax of the modern short story. ⁸How long is a short story? ⁹Edgar Allen Poe, a 19th century American writer, famously said that a short story should be short enough to be read at one sitting and should be focused on creating a single effect. ¹⁰In practice, most literary critics today put the length of a short story between about one thousand and twenty thousand words. ¹¹Anything shorter is called "flash fiction" or a "short-short," and a longer work is called a novella, or, if longer than about fifty thousand words, a novel.

Name: _____

Section_____ Date _____

SCORE: (Number correct) × 20 = _____%

MAIN IDEAS: Test C

The main ideas of the following paragraphs appear at different locations. Identify each main idea by filling in its sentence number in the space provided.

____ 1. [1]Most non-human mammals demonstrate only a passing interest in the dead of their own species. [2]Lions will generally sniff or lick another dead lion before beginning to eat the body; chimpanzees will try to interact with their dead friends and relatives only until their bodies start to decompose. [3]Elephants, however, are unique among non-human mammals in that they appear to actually mourn their dead. [4]When presented with the dead body of another elephant, elephants will generally become agitated and upset, and caress the carcass with their trunks and feet. [5]In experiments in which elephants have been shown the skulls of a rhinoceros, a buffalo, and another elephant, they have demonstrated interest in only the elephant skull, gently touching and investigating it with their trunks and feet in much the same way they would a fellow elephant. [6]They also appear to be able to distinguish even very small pieces of ivory (elephant tusk) from other substances such as wood and rocks, for when presented with all three substances, elephants are overwhelmingly drawn to, and become agitated over, the ivory. [7]Animal scientists interpret these patterns of behavior as evidence that elephants are in mourning.

____ 2. [1]To a degree unknown to moderns, the resident of the preindustrial city literally was what he wore. [2]The Roman citizen, for example, expressed the fact of his citizenship by wearing, as decreed by law, the white toga. [3]A "gentleman" in the Colonial cities of America was known by his powdered wig. [4]The cap of the medieval Frenchman was made of velvet for the upper classes, rough cloth for the poor. [5]In Elizabethan England commoners were prohibited by law from wearing clothing fashioned from gold or silver cloth, velvet, furs, and other "luxury" materials. [6]Hair length also indicated status. [7]Among the Franks, only the elite had long hair. [8]The clothing of outcast groups was often regulated by law. [9]The Parsi minority in the Persian city of Yezd were forced, until the 1880s, to twist their turbans instead of folding them, were denied various colors, and were prohibited from wearing or carrying rings, umbrellas, and other items. [10]Occupation, too, was signaled by dress. [11]The lawyers of medieval France, for example, were distinguished by their round caps, and the executioners of the period were forced to wear a special coat of red or gold so that they would be readily recognizable in a crowd. [12]Each of the various types of traveling peddlers of Peking wore a distinctive costume, as did the clergy of twelfth-century Europe and the members of religious sects in numerous preindustrial cities.

_____ 3. [1]Born to a wealthy German American family in 1856, L. Frank Baum grew up in upstate New York. [2]His father had made a great deal of money from the oil industry, particularly Pennsylvania gushers that yielded a distinctive emerald-green oil. [3]The younger Baum was drawn to what he called the "dream life," with its guilt-free indulgence in pleasure. [4]Together with his wife, he founded a theater troupe that toured the Midwest in the 1880s. [5]There, he also became editor of the town newspaper, the Aberdeen _Saturday Pioneer_. [6]Baum eventually moved his family to Chicago, where he embarked on a career as a department-store window designer. [7]He founded the National Association of Window Trimmers in 1898 and started a trade magazine, _The Show Window_. [8]The magazine encouraged designers to strive for a "sumptuous display" of goods and to highlight their rich textures and colors. [9]Baum went on to become a popular writer of children's fiction. [10]His famous book _The Wizard of Oz_ (1900) is a brilliantly imaginative account of a Kansas farm girl's adventures "over the rainbow." [11]An accomplished and successful showman, L. Frank Baum understood that Americans were eager to buy fantasy wherever they could find it: in a theater, department store, or children's book.

_____ 4. [1]Everyone knows that the Ford Edsel was one of the most spectacular marketing flops in history, but not everyone agrees why. [2]The car was introduced to the public with much fanfare in 1957, but sales were disappointing and the model was abandoned by Ford after only three years. [3]Some say that the car was over-hyped from the beginning. [4]One of the biggest advance publicity campaigns in history kept the appearance of the car shrouded in mystery, and it could not possibly live up to expectations. [5]Others say that the distinctive "horse collar" grill was just plain ugly. [6]Still others insist it was the name that was ugly, and that the public would never warm to a car with the odd first name of former company president Edsel Ford. [7]There were also quality control problems, as Ford did not build an Edsel factory, but made it with parts made in Ford and Mercury factories. [8]While all of these arguments may have some validity, the biggest factor might not have had anything to do with the car itself, but with the fact that it was introduced during an economic recession. [9]The Edsel may have been short-lived, but the Ford Motor Company survived. [10]The same cannot be said of Hudson, Nash, Packard, and DeSoto, four distinguished car companies that went out of business between 1957 and 1960. [11]Nevertheless, it is the poor Edsel whose name is forever linked with new product disaster.

In paragraph 5, either of two sentences can be seen as the main idea. Identify one of them.

_____ 5. [1]Sigmund Freud is often called the father of psychoanalysis. [2]While his theories may be widely disputed today, he introduced many terms and concepts that are still in common usage. [3]Freud, who lived from 1856 to 1939, mainly in Vienna, Austria, developed theories of the unconscious mind. [4]Freud said that the human psyche has three parts. [5]He named them the id, the ego, and the superego. [6]The id represents unconscious drives that are repressed by people. [7]These drives, according to Freud, are primarily sexual. [8]The superego represents the moral judgment or the conscience. [9]The ego is the part that operates in the world and is mostly conscious. [10]The ego must deal with the drives of the id and the judgment of the superego. [11]The ego has what he called "defense mechanisms" to solve conflicts between the other two. [12]These defense mechanisms include denial, projection, and rationalization. [13]Dreams were important to Freud, as for him they represent outflowings of things the ego would rather keep hidden from the self. [14]Since his death, Freud's theories have come under a great deal of criticism. [15]While most psychologists no longer subscribe to his theories, his enormous influence in the history, literature, and culture of the 20th century cannot be denied.

Name: _____

Section_____ Date _____

SCORE: (Number correct) × 20 = _____%

MAIN IDEAS: Test D

The main ideas of the following paragraphs appear at different locations. Identify each main idea by filling in its sentence number in the space provided.

____ 1. [1]Mercury, also known as quicksilver, is one of the few elements that is in liquid form at room temperature. [2]Over the centuries mercury has had many ritualistic and scientific uses, almost all of which have been discontinued as its toxic properties have come to be understood. [3]In ancient China and India, mercury was considered an aid to good health. [4]Historians believe that an early Chinese emperor was driven insane and killed by mercury pills that were supposed to make him live forever. [5]In Europe and America in the 18th and 19th centuries, mercury was used in the manufacture of felt for making hats. [6]The mercury solution that the hat makers used was highly toxic. [7]Symptoms included hallucinations and dementia; thus the origin of the phrase "mad as a hatter." [8]Mercury was once widely used to treat syphilis, which caused confusion because mercury poisoning symptoms are so similar to those of the disease it was supposed to relieve. [9]It was also used as a diuretic and as a laxative. [10]Although now banned in the United States, mercurochrome is still widely used around the world as a topical antiseptic. [11]Mercury's use has been discontinued in home thermometers, herbicides, and light switches. [12]Through its industrial uses it has entered the food chain, showing up in potentially dangerous concentrations in some kinds of fish. [13]Mercury is still used in dentistry. [14]Although mercury amalgam fillings are still officially considered safe for humans, this usage has become controversial.

____ 2. [1]When people in organizations are asked, "Which skills most need to be strengthened?" they often voice strong opinions. [2]Several years ago, *Fortune* magazine surveyed many successful corporate executives to determine what subjects business schools should teach. [3]The answer hits home: "Teach them to write better," said executive after executive. [4]Another report indicates that "according to surveys of top officials in major American corporations, the greatest need among managers at all levels is to become more effective speakers and writers. . . . [5]The time and money wasted—not to mention the clients lost—by poor writing are staggering in scope." [6]Coopers & Lybrand, a prestigious accounting firm, is in such desperate need of good proposal writers that it has considered hiring English majors and providing them with on-the-job training in accounting. [7]Clearly, the experience of business executives suggests that American schools should do a better job of teaching communication skills.

____ 3. [1]Do you ever wish you could shut off your brain, stop worrying about your problems, and just sleep for a few days? [2]If you could, you'd have a lot in common with animals that hibernate during the winter. [3]Hibernating animals, scientists have learned, actually switch off their brain cells for a week or more during winter months, and recent research suggests that studying how these animals do this may allow us to help people with brain damage brought on by strokes. [4]Investigations into the brain of the American ground squirrel, for instance, show that parts of the squirrel's brain actually start to disappear once he's gone into hibernation. [5]The squirrel's brain cells, which resemble large bushes, each begin to shrink, or pull in their branches, until between 20 and 40 percent of the original brain structure is lost. [6]A person who suffers a severe stroke, or a loss of blood to the brain cells, might experience a similar amount of brain loss. [7]What scientists have discovered about the ground squirrel, however, is that between three and four hours after he wakes up, his brain has completely grown back again, and he continues to live his life exactly as he did before he went into hibernation. [8]Severe stroke victims, by contrast, usually manage to recover only a small fraction of their lost brain structure—and even then, it can take months or even years to make this much progress. [9]Researchers are thus hoping that doctors will eventually be able to reproduce a hibernation-like state in the brains of people suffering from strokes to help them regrow the brain cells they have lost.

____ 4. [1]The national park system, one of America's greatest creations, owes much of its success to a painter and to a president. [2]In feudal Europe, certain lands were set aside for preservation, usually as royal hunting grounds owned by the king. [3]The national parks, on the other hand, are owned by all Americans. [4]A 19th century painter named George Catlin contributed much to the origin of national parks. [5]He traveled widely in the American West, painting portraits of native Americans and landscapes of the most beautiful natural wonders. [6]Catlin argued for a government policy to protect certain pristine areas. [7]In 1864, Catlin saw his dream come to life when Congress donated the Yosemite area to the state of California for preservation as a state park. [8]In 1872 Yellowstone became the first national park. [9]Theodore Roosevelt, president from 1901 to 1909, gave a great boost to conservation, setting aside more land for national parks and national preserves than all his predecessors combined, about 194 million acres. [10]Today there are fifty-eight national parks. [11]The largest, Wrangell-St. Elias National Park in Alaska, with more than thirteen million acres, is five times the size of Yellowstone. [12]Only one national park is named for a president. [13]That one, dedicated to preserving the unique geography of the Badlands of North Dakota, is the Theodore Roosevelt National Park.

____ 5. [1]The list of the ten deadliest animals, as determined by the group Live Science, contains many of the fearsome killers you'd expect, and a few that you've probably never heard of. [2]African lions, number five on the list, and great white sharks, number four, are well known for their killer instincts. [3]Few people ever choose to tangle with an Australian saltwater crocodile, number six, or a 16,000-pound African elephant, number seven. [4]More than 50,000 people die every year from snakebite, and the leading assassin in the snake world is the Asian cobra, which puts it at number two. [5]You'd have to be in some very specific corners of the world to run afoul of a cape buffalo, number nine, or a polar bear, number eight. [6]One deadly creature that you might not expect to find on the list is the poison dart frog, number ten. [7]Don't pet the cute amphibian, however, because the slime on its back is deadly enough to kill ten people. [8]The Australian box jellyfish is beautiful and graceful in the water, but each of its many fifteen-foot-long tentacles has enough toxins to kill sixty humans, which puts it all the way up at number 3. [9]The most deadly animal of all is not exotic. [10]In fact, you have probably done battle with it many times. [11]Nevertheless, it's responsible for millions of deaths every year by infecting people with the parasites that cause malaria. [12]Yes, the most deadly animal on the planet is the mosquito.

Name: _____

Section_____ Date _____

SCORE: (Number correct) × 10 = _____%

SUPPORTING DETAILS: Test A

A. (1–5.) Answer the supporting-detail questions that follow the textbook passage.

> [1]Conflict is an inevitable part of every person's life. [2]Everyone deals with conflict in a more or less individual manner. [3]At the same time, five general patterns of reacting to conflict can be identified. [4]One such pattern is withdrawal, the physical or psychological removal from a conflict situation. [5]Another manner of dealing with conflict is surrender, giving in immediately to another's wishes in order to avoid an argument. [6]Aggression is a third way to deal with conflict. [7]Those favoring aggressive behavior try to force other people to accept the aggressor's opinions. [8]Conflict also can be dealt with through persuasion, or attempting to change the behavior or attitude of another person. [9]A final means of dealing with conflict is discussion, or verbal problem solving, in which the pros and cons of the issue in conflict are weighed and considered.

____ 1. Sentence 3 provides
   A. the main idea.
   B. a major detail.
   C. a minor detail.

____ 2. Sentence 5 provides
   A. the main idea.
   B. a major detail.
   C. a minor detail.

____ 3. Sentence 7 provides
   A. the main idea.
   B. a major detail.
   C. a minor detail.

____ 4. The fourth major detail of the paragraph is introduced in sentence
   A. 7.
   B. 8.
   C. 9.

5. *Fill in the blank:* One addition word that introduces a major supporting detail is

_____.

B. (6–10.) Complete the map of the following textbook passage by filling in the main idea and the missing major supporting details.

¹An ideology is a consistent pattern of opinion on particular issues that stems from a core or basic belief. ²In America, generally speaking, there are four major ideological types. ³One type, conservatives, are defined as individuals who oppose an activist role for government in providing economic benefits but look to government to uphold traditional social values. ⁴In contrast, liberals favor activist government as an instrument of economic redistribution but reject the notion that government should favor a particular set of social values. ⁵True liberals and conservatives could be expected to differ, for instance, on the issues of homosexual rights (a social-values question) and government-guaranteed health care (an economic-distribution question). ⁶Liberals would view homosexuality as a private issue and believe that government should ensure that everyone has access to adequate medical care. ⁷Conservatives would oppose government-mandated access to health care and favor government policies that actively discourage homosexual lifestyles. ⁸A third major ideological type are Populists, who are defined as individuals who share with conservatives a concern for traditional values, but like liberals, favor an active role for government in providing economic security. ⁹Finally, libertarians are opposed to government intervention in both the economic and social spheres.

Main idea: _____

_____ .

_____ :	_____ :	_____ :	_____ :

Name: _____

Section_____ Date _____

SCORE: (Number correct) × 10 = _____%

SUPPORTING DETAILS: Test B

A. (1–5.) Answer the supporting-detail questions that follow the passage below.

[1]In the 1950s, stunned by television's popularity, the movie business tried various ways to lure its audience back. [2]One way was by filming some movies in 3-D, using special effects to create the illusion of three-dimensional action. [3]Rocks, for example, seemed to fly off the screen and into the audience. [4]To see the 3-D movies, people wore special plastic glasses. [5]The novelty was fun, but the 3-D movie plots were weak, and most people didn't come back to see a second 3-D movie. [6]Another way that movies tried to regain audiences was with the use of Cinerama, Cinemascope, VistaVision and Panavision—wide-screen color movies with stereophonic sound. [7]Movie producers hoped that wide-screen technology would highlight the contrast between the viewing experience in theaters and the viewing experience at home. [8]Finally, Hollywood studios began concentrating on filming spectaculars—expensive big-screen epics that featured large, star-studded casts. [9]*Ben-Hur*, *The Sound of Music,* and *The Godfather* are prime examples of big-budget movies that succeeded in offering viewers something that television couldn't.

____ 1. Sentence 1 provides
   A. the main idea.
   B. a major detail.
   C. a minor detail.

____ 2. The major supporting details of this paragraph are
   A. advances in film technology.
   B. reasons why movies declined in popularity.
   C. ways that the movie industry tried to regain customers.

____ 3. Sentence 5 provides
   A. the main idea.
   B. a major detail.
   C. a minor detail.

____ 4. How many major supporting details does the paragraph include?
   A. Two
   B. Three
   C. Four

5. *Fill in the blank:* One addition word that introduces a major supporting detail is

_____.

B. (6–10.) Complete the map of the following textbook passage by adding the main idea and the missing major details.

[1]New information technology is drawing nations of the world closer together, creating a global economy, expanding economic activity with little regard for national borders. [2]The development of a global economy has four major consequences. [3]First, we see a global division of labor, so that different regions of the world specialize in one or another sector of economic activity. [4]For instance, agriculture represents more than half of the total economic output in the world's poorest countries, while most of the economic output in high-income countries is in the service sector. [5]Second, an increasing number of products pass through more than one nation. [6]Look no further than your morning coffee, which may well have been grown in Colombia and transported to New Orleans on a freighter that was registered in Liberia, made in Japan using steel from Korea, and fueled by oil from Venezuela.

[7]A third consequence of the global economy is that national governments no longer control the economic activity that takes place within their borders. [8]In fact, governments cannot even regulate the value of their national currencies because dollars, euros, pounds sterling, yen, and other currencies are traded around the clock in the financial centers of Tokyo, London, and New York. [9]The fourth consequence of the global economy is that a small number of businesses, operating internationally, now control a vast share of the world's economic activity. [10]According to one estimate, the 600 largest multinational companies account for half the world's entire economic output.

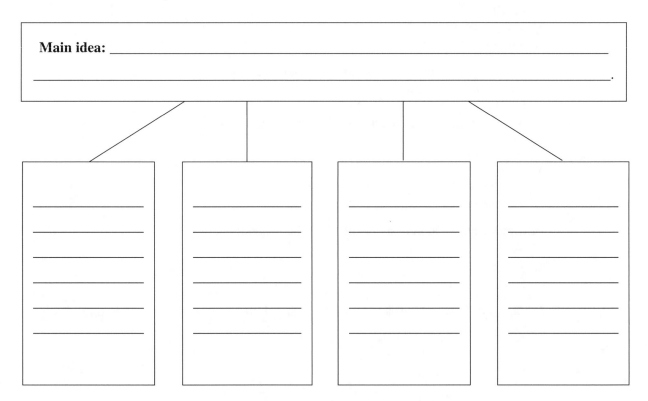

Main idea: _____

_____.

SUPPORTING DETAILS: Test C

A. (1–5.) Answer the supporting-detail questions that follow the passage below.

¹In any vital city, a sidewalk has uses far beyond easing the passage of pedestrians. ²Front steps facing the sidewalk are places for neighbors to sit and visit, just as corners are places to "hang out." ³Sidewalk street life also serves as a means of public surveillance, through which people come to know each other and to identify strangers. ⁴Sociologist Jane Jacobs points out that in areas where street life abounds, crime rates are low. ⁵In addition, sidewalks are environments where children explore their neighborhood, test themselves, and grasp the rules of urban social life. ⁶Finally, street life brings a sense of community to a neighborhood. ⁷South Philadelphia, New York's Lower East Side, New Orleans's French Quarter, and San Francisco's Haight-Ashbury district all maintain a positive identity based on their street life.

____ 1. Sentence 1 provides
    A. the main idea.
    B. a major detail.
    C. a minor detail.

____ 2. Sentence 2 provides
    A. the main idea.
    B. a major detail.
    C. a minor detail.

____ 3. Sentence 4 provides
    A. the main idea.
    B. a major detail.
    C. a minor detail.

____ 4. The third major detail of the paragraph is introduced in sentence
    A. 3.
    B. 4.
    C. 5.

____ 5. The fourth major detail is signaled with the addition word(s)
    A. *also.*
    B. *In addition.*
    C. *Finally.*

B. (6–10.) Complete the map of the following textbook passage by filling in the main idea and the missing major supporting details.

¹The British Empire banned slavery in 1833; the United States followed suit in 1865. ²But according to Anti-Slavery International (ASI), as many as 400 million men, women, and children (almost 7 percent of humanity) live today in conditions that amount to slavery. ³ASI distinguishes four types of slavery. ⁴First is chattel slavery, in which one person owns another. ⁵The number of chattel slaves is difficult to estimate because the practice is against the law almost everywhere. ⁶But the buying and selling of slaves still takes place in many countries in Asia, the Middle East, and especially Africa. ⁷A second, more common form of bondage is child slavery, in which desperately poor families let their children take to the streets to do what they can to survive. ⁸Perhaps 100 million children—many in poor countries of Latin America—fall into this category. ⁹Third, debt bondage is the practice by which employers hold workers captive by paying them too little to meet their debts. ¹⁰In this case, workers receive a wage, but it is too small to cover the food and housing provided by an employer; for practical purposes, they are enslaved. ¹¹Many workers in sweatshops fall into this category. ¹²Finally, servile forms of marriage may also amount to slavery. ¹³In India, Thailand, and some African nations, families marry off women against their will. ¹⁴Many end up as slaves performing work for their husband's family; some are forced into prostitution.

Main idea: _____
_____.

```
       _____:        _____:        _____:        _____:
       _____         _____         _____         _____
       _____         _____         _____         _____
       _____         _____         _____         _____
       _____         _____         _____         _____
```

SUPPORTING DETAILS: Test D

A. (1–5.) Answer the supporting-detail questions that follow the passage below.

¹In education, as in other fields, new technologies tend to go through three stages of application. ²In the first stage, the technology is applied to things we already do. ³For instance, when microcomputer programs were first introduced into education, computer programs were created to simulate flash cards for math drill. ⁴As a technology moves into the second stage, it is used to improve on the tasks we do. ⁵As an example, a more sophisticated math software application can provide remedial instruction when a student makes the same mistake more than once. ⁶It can also expand to cover more math topics and increase motivation by using gamelike activities. ⁷In the final stage of maturity, the technology is used to do things that were not possible before. ⁸An example of technology in this stage would be a geographic information system (GIS) which can translate data to a digital map. ⁹The power of a GIS comes from its ability to display several layers of maps on a computer screen at a single time. ¹⁰This kind of application enables students to pull together their knowledge and skills from disciplines in a collaborative manner to solve a problem in their local communities.

____ 1. The main idea is expressed in sentence
   A. 1.
   B. 2.
   C. 3.

____ 2. The major supporting details of this paragraph are
   A. results.
   B. characteristics.
   C. stages.

____ 3. Sentence 3 contains
   A. the main idea.
   B. a major detail.
   C. a minor detail.

____ 4. Sentences 5–6 contain
   A. major supporting details.
   B. minor supporting details.

   5. *Fill in the blank*: One addition word that introduces a major supporting detail is

   _____.

B. (6–10.) Answer the supporting-detail questions that follow the passage below.

[1]In the next fifteen years, the population of people over the age of fifty in the United States will soar upward by 75 percent. [2]During the same period, the number of people under the age of fifty will increase by just 2 percent. [3]There are two reasons for this rapid aging of our society. [4]The first is the baby boom that began in the late 1940s. [5]With the end of World War II, men and women quickly settled into family life and, by 1965, had some 75 million babies. [6]This enormous population boom led to the youth culture of the 1960s. [7]And as the baby boomers continue to age, they will produce an "elder boom" which is expected to peak around 2025. [8]The second explanation for the aging of our society is increasing life expectancy. [9]Improvements in medicine and nutrition have resulted in people living longer than ever. [10]Newborns today can expect to live thirty years longer than those born in 1900. [11]The sharp and recent increase in the number of elderly people—here and around the world—supports the surprising fact that more than half of all the elderly people who have ever lived are alive today.

_____ 6. The main idea is expressed in sentence
   A. 1.
   B. 2.
   C. 3.

_____ 7. The major supporting details of this paragraph are
   A. results.
   B. reasons.
   C. characteristics.

_____ 8. The first major detail of the paragraph is introduced in sentence
   A. 3.
   B. 4.
   C. 5.

_____ 9. The second major detail of the paragraph is introduced in sentence
   A. 6.
   B. 7.
   C. 8.

_____ 10. Sentences 9–11 contain
   A. major supporting details.
   B. minor supporting details.

Name: _____

Section_____ Date _____

SCORE: (Number correct) × 25 = _____%

IMPLIED MAIN IDEAS: Test A

In the space provided, write the letter of the sentence that best expresses the implied main idea of each of the following paragraphs.

____ 1. [1]Fifty years ago, public libraries were, for the most part, rather no-frills places. [2]There were shelves of books, a rack of well-thumbed magazines, and a tight-lipped librarian behind a desk who commanded everyone to speak in a whisper, if at all. [3]Today's libraries, however, are exciting and adaptable "media centers" where people of all ages come to select from among a vast and constantly changing array of books, magazines, audio books, videos, CDs, and DVDs. [4]In addition, today's libraries often feature computers with Internet hookups and kiosks where patrons may refresh themselves with their favorite beverage or snack. [5]And the librarians, too, are a far cry from yesterday's rigid relics. [6]Most likely, they are people who are at home with the latest information technologies and, thus, happy to share their expertise.

    A. Today's libraries offer a wide variety of books, magazines, audio books, videos, CDs, and DVDs.
    B. Librarians have changed greatly in the past fifty years.
    C. Today's libraries cater to people of all ages.
    D. Today's libraries are pleasingly different from what they were fifty years ago.

____ 2. [1]Far from being America's favorite food, during the early 1900s, hamburgers were considered "food for the poor." [2]Restaurants generally didn't sell them. [3]Burgers were served at lunch carts parked near factories, at circuses, and at carnivals. [4]It was widely believed that ground beef was made from rotten old meat full of chemical preservatives. [5]In the mid-1920s, however, a man named Walt Anderson set out to defend the hamburger from its many critics. [6]Walt loved burgers and opened a small restaurant devoted to selling them—the first White Castle—in Wichita, Kansas. [7]Walt grilled the burgers right in front of his customers, so they could see for themselves that the meat and the equipment were clean. [8]He also supported an unusual experiment at the University of Minnesota. [9]For thirteen weeks, a medical student there consumed nothing but White Castle hamburgers and water. [10]When the student not only survived the experiment but also seemed pretty healthy, people started to view hamburgers in a new light. [11]Now hamburgers seemed wholesome, not deadly.

    A. For many years, hamburgers were viewed as being unhealthy.
    B. Walt Anderson, the founder of the first White Castle, made people finally realize that hamburgers were safe to eat.
    C. By grilling hamburgers in the open, Walt Anderson proved to people that hamburgers were safe to eat.
    D. Not all hamburgers are safe to eat.

_____ 3. [1]Working at home is convenient and flexible and can be less stressful than daily commuting. [2]It can benefit employers (who need less space), employees (who save on clothing and transportation), and entrepreneurs (who save on office expenses). [3]However, it is not for everyone: it requires enough initiative, independence, and self-confidence to work without supervision. [4]Some home workers feel isolated or have trouble concentrating in the presence of such distractions as television, the refrigerator, and young children. [5]Also, employees who work at home may lose fringe benefits, such as health insurance, and the protection of laws guaranteeing fair labor standards and working conditions.

    A. Working at home is convenient, flexible, and less stressful than daily commuting.
    B. Working at home has both advantages and disadvantages.
    C. Working at home requires enough initiative, independence, and self-confidence to work without supervision.
    D. Although working at home can be convenient and flexible, employees who work at home may lose valuable fringe benefits.

_____ 4. [1]In ancient Rome, a left-handed boy who was training to be a soldier would have his hand bound to his side, and would be forced to use his weapon with his right hand. [2]In the early Catholic Church, left-handedness was often interpreted as a sign of Satanic influence, and thus prohibited. [3]Many examples can be found in the Christian-Greek Scriptures in which the wicked or evil sit at the left hand of God, while the righteous sit at the right hand of God, during the Last Judgment. [4]Until the latter part of the twentieth century, Roman Catholic nuns in United States elementary schools would punish children for using their left hand to write, typically by slapping their left hand with a ruler if they attempted to pick up a pen with it. [5]An example of such treatment involves baseball players Lou Gehrig and Babe Ruth, who both hit and threw left-handed and wrote right-handed after being forced to do so during their formative years. [6]Also, until very recently, in Chinese societies, left-handed people were strongly encouraged to switch to being right-handed. [7]However, this may be in part because, while Latin characters are equally easy to write with either hand, it is more difficult to write legible Chinese characters with the left hand

    A. It is possible to train left-handed people to become right-handed.
    B. Most cultures have looked upon left-handed people as wicked.
    C. Left-handedness has been frowned upon in many cultures.
    D. The Catholic Church used to consider left-handed people wicked.

Name: _____

Section_____ Date _____

SCORE: (Number correct) × 25 = _____%

IMPLIED MAIN IDEAS: Test B

In the space provided, write the letter of the sentence that best expresses the implied main idea of each of the following paragraphs.

____ 1. [1]For many years the University of Chicago's National Opinion Research Center has asked respondents whether they think the federal government is spending too much, too little, or about the right amount of money on "assistance for the poor." [2]Answering the question posed this way, about two-thirds of all respondents seem to believe that the government is spending too little. [3]However, the same survey also asks whether the government spends too much, too little, or about the right amount for "welfare." [4]When the word "welfare" is substituted for "assistance for the poor," about half of all respondents indicate that too much is being spent by the government.

    A. Chicago's National Opinion Research Center is a leader in conducting public opinion research.
    B. Most Americans believe that the government spends too much money on welfare.
    C. In opinion polls, how a question is phrased can affect the answers people give.
    D. Most people want the United States government to give more assistance to the poor.

____ 2. [1]In species such as the red-back spider, the black widow spider, the praying mantis, and the scorpion, the female commonly eats the male after mating. [2]Another widespread form of cannibalism is size-structured cannibalism, in which large individuals consume smaller ones. [3]Octopus, bats, toads, fish, monitor lizards, salamanders, crocodiles, spiders, crustaceans, birds, mammals, and a vast number of insects have all been observed to engage in size-structured cannibalism. [4]Yet another common form of cannibalism is infanticide. [5]Classical examples include the chimpanzees, where groups of adult males have been observed to attack and consume their infants; and lions, where adult males commonly kill infants when they take over a new harem after replacing the previous dominant males. [6]Also, gerbils and hamsters eat their young if they are stillborn, or if the mothers are especially stressed.

    A. Cannibalism is common in the animal world.
    B. Most animals engage in cannibalism.
    C. Not only insects, but lizards and mammals engage in cannibalism.
    D. Size-structured cannibalism is the most common form of cannibalism.

_____ 3. [1]T-shirts can function as trophies (as proof of participation in sports or travel) or as self-proclaimed labels of belonging to a cultural category ("Super Bowl XXV Attendee," "Retired"). [2]T-shirts can also be used as a means of self-expression, which may provide wearers with the additional benefit of serving as a "topic" initiating social dialogue with others. [3]Still further, although we might expect that a Las Vegas T-shirt would be worn by a person who has been to Las Vegas (or has received it as a gift from someone else who has visited Las Vegas), this is not necessarily so. [4]In such a world of "virtual identities," consumers can now just buy a Las Vegas T-shirt at a local retailer and create the impression that they have been there.

A. People often wear T-shirts to convey a false impression of themselves.
B. Many people wear T-shirts in the hope that in so doing, they will be able to initiate social dialogue with others.
C. T-shirts have a variety of functions.
D. T-shirts are a means of self-expression.

_____ 4. [1]Are men also victims of domestic violence? [2]Some women do abuse and even kill their partners. [3]Approximately 12 percent of men reported that their wives had engaged in physically aggressive behavior against them in the past year—nearly the same percentage of claims reported from women. [4]The difference between male and female batterers is twofold. [5]First, although the frequency may be similar, the impact is drastically different: women are typically injured in domestic incidents two to three times more often than are men. [6]These injuries tend to be more severe and have resulted in significantly more deaths. [7]Women do engage in moderate aggression, such as pushing and shoving at rates almost equal to those of men. [8]But severe aggression that is likely to land a victim in the hospital is almost always male against female. [9]Second, a woman who is physically abused by a man is generally intimidated by him; she fears that he will use his power and control over her in some fashion. [10]Men, however, generally report that they do not live in fear of their wives.

A. Men report that their wives have engaged in physically aggressive behavior against them at about the same rate that women report being abused by men.
B. Although some men are victims of domestic violence, in general women are more damaged by domestic violence than men are.
C. Men are generally not intimidated by their wives, even when their wives engage in moderate aggression.
D. Men inflict greater injuries upon women than women do upon men.

IMPLIED MAIN IDEAS: Test C

In the space provided, write the letter of the sentence that best expresses the implied main idea of each of the following paragraphs.

_____ 1. [1]In ancient Greece, homosexual love was prized above heterosexual relationships. [2]Greek men fell in love with teenage boys and inscribed passionate notes to them on urns; the poet Sappho wrote graphically of her physical arousal when she saw the woman she loved. [3]In some cultures, love has been separated from sexuality. [4]In King Arthur's court, love involved a nonsexual chivalry rather than intimacy; knights undertook feats of bravery to impress fair ladies but didn't seek to marry them. [5]In the Roman Catholic Church, love of God is considered superior to love of a human being, and priests remain celibate so as to devote themselves completely to their calling. [6]In Victorian England, love was viewed as a noble emotion, but sexual intimacy was considered a necessary evil, required only for producing children. [7]The Victorian poets placed the beloved on a pedestal. [8]A more modern view is that of loving someone for the person he or she is, warts and all.

    A. In many cultures, sexual intimacy is viewed as a necessary evil.
    B. Within Western civilization, ideas about love have changed dramatically.
    C. Modern people have a more relaxed attitude toward love than people in ancient Greece and Victorian England.
    D. In most cultures, men seek to impress the women they love.

_____ 2. [1]In the 1490s, the astronomer Nicolaus Copernicus left his home in Torun and journeyed to the Polish university town of Krakow, where he became caught up in the debate over whether the Earth or the sun was the center of our planetary system. [2]According to the Catholic Church, God had created man in His own image and had naturally placed him in the center of the system. [3]A tidy, closed universe came to be the conventional wisdom, with Earth surrounded by crystallized rings containing the moon, sun, and planets; hovering outside the last ring were, of course, God and the angels. [4]At first, Copernicus worked on making the church's view on the nature of the universe simpler, yet mathematically precise. [5]However, the more Copernicus worked, the less he could defend Rome's position. [6]Finally, in 1543, in a book dedicated to Pope Paul III, he advanced his theory of a sun-centered (heliocentric), not human-centered (homocentric) universe. [7]It was criticized by the church and by Martin Luther and was considered suspicious by most of the astronomers of the time. [8]But by the end of the century, the Copernican hypothesis had been verified, and Europeans came to accept the notion that their old way of thinking had been turned upside down.

    A. For most of the 1500s, people believed that the Earth, not the sun, was the center of our planetary system.
    B. During the 1500s, Nicolaus Copernicus's theory that the sun is the center of our planetary system gradually gained acceptance.
    C. In the 1500s, Nicolaus Copernicus gradually lost faith in the belief that the sun revolved around the Earth.
    D. Most astronomers of the time viewed Nicolaus Copernicus and his heliocentric theory with suspicion.

____ 3. [1]Graphologists believe that studying a person's handwriting can reveal his or her temperament, personality traits, intelligence, and reasoning ability. [2]But can it? [3]Consider a recent study that investigated graphologists' ability to distinguish between people in three different groups: successful versus unsuccessful secretaries; successful business entrepreneurs versus librarians and bank clerks; and actors and actresses versus monks and nuns. [4]The three groups represented a combined total of 170 participants. [5]As requested by the graphologists, all participants indicated their age, sex, and hand preference. [6]Each person also produced 20 lines of spontaneous handwriting on a neutral topic. [7]Four leading graphologists independently evaluated each handwriting sample. [8]For each group, the graphologists tried to assign each handwriting sample to one category or another. [9]The handwriting samples were also analyzed by four ordinary people with no formal training in graphology or psychology. [10]When the results were in, the completely inexperienced judges achieved a success rate of 59 percent correct. [11]The professional graphologists achieved a slightly better success rate of 65 percent. [12]Obviously, this is not a great difference.

A. A recent study casts doubt on whether professional graphologists can really predict a person's personality traits, etc. on the basis of handwriting.
B. A recent study indicates that a person does not need specialized training to be able to accurately categorize people on the basis of their handwriting.
C. A recent study suggests that studying a person's handwriting is a highly reliable method of learning about their temperament, personality traits, intelligence, and reasoning ability.
D. A recent study confirms that professional graphologists can determine a person's temperament, personality traits, intelligence, and reasoning ability based upon his or her handwriting.

____ 4. [1]All of us have at one time or another been repelled by so-called agony commercials, which depict in graphic detail the internal and intestinal effects of heartburn, indigestion, clogged sinus cavities, hammer-induced headaches, and the like. [2]Nevertheless, pharmaceutical companies often run such commercials with great success because they appeal to a certain segment of the population that suffers from ailments that are not visible and thus elicit little sympathy from family and friends. [3]Their complaints are legitimized by commercials with which they immediately identify. [4]With the sponsor's credibility established ("They really understand the misery I'm going through"), the message itself tends to be highly persuasive in getting consumers to buy the advertised product.

A. Agony commercials are designed to appeal to a certain segment of the viewing public.
B. Most people find agony commercials disgusting.
C. Despite being repellent to many, agony commercials are generally successful.
D. Agony commercials detail the internal and intestinal effects of various ailments.

Name: _____

Section_____ Date _____

SCORE: (Number correct) × 25 = _____%

IMPLIED MAIN IDEAS: Test D

In the space provided, write the letter of the sentence that best expresses the implied main idea of each of the following paragraphs.

____ 1. [1]When Julius Caesar landed on the island we now know as Britain almost two thousand years ago, English didn't even exist. [2]Five hundred years later, a form of English called Old English (which was so different from modern English that you and I couldn't even understand it) had emerged, and was spoken by only a few thousand people. [3]By the time William Shakespeare was writing his greatest plays, in the late sixteenth century, English was the native language of five to seven million British people, but was not used anywhere outside of Britain itself. [4]In the four hundred years since then, English-speakers such as the Scottish, the Irish, the Americans, and many others have carried their language and culture to all parts of the globe, and English has become the most widely spoken, written, and far-reaching language in human history. [5]Today English is used by roughly a billion people, more than half of whom have learned it as a second language. [6]It has become a global language of business as well as technology, appearing in 75 percent of the world's mail and 80 percent of the information stored in the world's computers.

  A. Modern English is nothing like Old English, which was used about 1500 years ago.
  B. The Scottish, the Irish, and the Americans are among the peoples who have carried English to all parts of the globe.
  C. English has spread to become a global language of business and technology.
  D. Worldwide use of English has expanded greatly during the past few centuries.

____ 2. [1]The concept of nutrition has been around since the early 19th century, when the English doctor and chemist William Prout identified what came to be called the "macronutrients": protein, fat, and carbohydrates. [2]It was thought that that was pretty much all there was going on in food, until the doctors noticed than an adequate supply of the big three did not necessarily keep people nourished. [3]At the end of the 19th century, British doctors were puzzled by the fact that Chinese laborers in the Malay states were dying of a disease called beriberi, which didn't seem to afflict Tamils or native Malays. [4]The mystery was solved when someone pointed out that the Chinese ate "polished," or white, rice, while the others ate rice that hadn't been mechanically milled. [5]A few years later, Casimir Funk, a Polish chemist, discovered the "essential nutrient" in rice husks that protected against beriberi and called it a "vitamine," the first micronutrient.

  A. The "big three" nutrients are protein, fat, and carbohydrates.
  B. People who eat rice that has not been mechanically milled are generally healthier than people who eat "polished," or white rice.
  C. The concept of nutrition developed over two hundred years ago.
  D. In the late 19th century, it was discovered that micronutrients known as vitamins are essential to health.

_____ 3. [1]When Attila the Hun and his barbarian hordes swept across northern Italy in about 430 A.D., they wrought havoc and destruction on the remnants of the Roman Empire. [2]But they unintentionally left another, more positive legacy as well. [3]Refugees fled burning cities, desperate to find safe refuge. [4]Some literally took to the swamps, finding sanctuary in a desolate group of islands in a marshy lagoon off the northern Adriatic. [5]When the Huns were followed by other invading tribes, more Roman citizens streamed to the swamps to avoid the carnage and destruction on the mainland. [6]Over the next few centuries, they transformed the inhospitable surroundings into an architectural wonder: Venice. [7]With more than four hundred bridges and almost two hundred canals, the city on the lagoon became a center of trade and a seafaring power. [8]By the thirteenth century, Venice was the most prosperous city in all of Europe. [9]Today it remains one of the most beautiful (and visited) cities in the world.

A. Venice was founded on islands in a marshy lagoon around the year 430 AD.
B. Although it began on a desolate group of islands off the northern Adriatic, Venice eventually became a great city.
C. The Huns and other invading tribes caused Roman refugees to stream to a desolate group of islands off the northern Adriatic.
D. In the 400s, refugees fleeing barbarian tribes settled on swampy ground off the northern Adriatic.

_____ 4. [1]In 1818, British author Mary Shelley wrote what was probably the world's first science-fiction novel, _Frankenstein_. [2]In the novel, scientist Victor Frankenstein sets out to create a man by piecing together the remains of corpses gathered in charnel houses. [3]While his efforts prove successful, Victor is revolted by the ugliness of the man he has created and abandons it. [4]Enraged by his creator's abandonment, the creature becomes a killer and wrecks havoc upon all those Victor holds dear. [5]Victor goes in pursuit of his creation, and both eventually die in the barren wastes near the North Pole. [6]In 1886, Robert Louis Stevenson published the _Strange Case of Dr. Jekyll and Mr. Hyde_. [7]In this story, a mild-mannered London physician, bored with his life, creates a potion that when swallowed frees his evil twin, Edward Hyde. [8]A living embodiment of Jekyll's repressed desires, Hyde runs wild, kills a member of Parliament, becomes a fugitive, and eventually destroys both himself and his creator. [9]More recently, American author Michael Crichton's _Jurassic Park_ tells what happens when modern scientists clone dinosaurs using the DNA found in the remains of prehistoric mosquitoes. [10]Predictably enough, the dinosaurs run out of control, killing the organizers of the theme park which was to "safely" display them, while two paleontologists are among those who narrowly escape with their lives.

A. Modern-day scientists engage in all sorts of crazy experiments which end up causing more harm than good.
B. The dangers of tampering with nature in the interests of science have been a recurring theme in literature for the past two hundred years.
C. In 1818, Mary Shelley wrote the world's first science fiction novel, _Frankenstein_; that, in turn, has led to many other works of science fiction.
D. Both British and American authors have written hugely successful science fiction novels.

RELATIONSHIPS I: Test A

A. Fill in each blank with an appropriate transition from the box. Use each transition once. Then, in the space provided, write the letter of the transition you have chosen.

A. also	B. finally	C. in addition
D. later	E. until	

____ 1. [1]One way to avoid tempting car thieves is by locking all valuables in the trunk or glove compartment. [2]You can _____ discourage thieves with tow trucks by parking in the middle of a block on a busy, well-lit street.

____ 2. [1]The earliest humans probably used the lengthening and shortening of shadows on the ground to measure the passage of time. [2]_____, the sundial was invented to tell time more precisely, but still by using the shadow principle.

____ 3. [1]According to some researchers, passionate love will not occur unless three conditions are met. [2]First, the person must live in a culture in which the concept of "falling in love" is idealized. [3]Second, a "suitable" love object must be present. [4]If someone has been taught by parents, movies, books, and peers to seek partners of a certain appearance, socioeconomic status, or racial background, and if no such partner is available, the person may find it difficult to become involved. [5]_____, there must be some type of physiological arousal that occurs when a person is in the presence of the beloved. [6]Often this arousal takes the form of sexual excitement.

____ 4. [1]Babies respond to the same four categories of tastes (sweet, sour, bitter, and salty) as adults do. [2]_____, they can identify familiar body odors and can even discriminate their mother's smell from the smell of another woman.

____ 5. [1]The motion picture, invented in 1889, developed as an important form of entertainment during the first decade of the twentieth century. [2]At first, the "nickelodeons," as the early movie theaters were called, appealed mainly to a lower-class and largely ethnic audience. [3]In 1902, New York City had 50 theaters; by 1908, there were more than 400 showing 30-minute dramas and romances. [4]Not _____ World War I, when D.W. Griffith produced long feature films, did the movies begin to attract a middle-class audience.

B. (6–9.) Fill in each blank with an appropriate transition from the box. Use each transition once.

A. during D. when	B. first	C. second

[1]During the (6)_____, or dilation, stage of the birth process, the uterus contracts, and the cervix flattens and dilates to allow the fetus to pass through. [2]This labor stage can last from about two to sixteen hours, or even longer; it tends to be longer with the first child. [3](7)_____ the contractions start, they usually come at approximately fifteen- to twenty-minute intervals and are generally mild. [4]Near the end of this first stage, the contractions change, becoming more difficult, longer, and more frequent. [5]This period, lasting about an hour, is called "transition" and is the most difficult part of labor for many women. [6]The (8)_____ stage of birth involves the actual delivery of the baby. [7]This expulsion stage is quite variable and can last anywhere from two to sixty minutes or more. [8]In the average delivery, the baby's head appears first, an event referred to as crowning. [9]The rest of the body soon follows. [10]The third stage of the birth process involves the delivery of the placenta (or afterbirth) and fetal membranes. [11](9)_____ this stage, mild contractions continue for some time. [12]They help decrease the blood flow to the uterus and reduce the uterus to normal size.

____ 10. The pattern of organization of the above selection is
    A. list of items.
    B. time order.

RELATIONSHIPS I: Test B

A. Fill in each blank with an appropriate transition from the box. Use each transition once. Then, in the space provided, write the letter of the transition you have chosen.

A. during	B. in addition	C. last of all
D. second	E. when	

____ 1. [1]Hay fever is a genetic abnormality; it runs in families. [2]Some individuals simply are genetically predisposed to overreact to certain kinds of pollen. [3]_____, infections, emotional stress, and changes in temperature may trigger immune reactions to pollen.

____ 2. [1]Sociologists have several basic methods of doing research. [2]First is the experiment, which is useful for clearly defined questions in which varying factors can be controlled. [3]A _____ method sociologists use is the survey, which is useful for gaining facts about a particular group; in order to be sound, the survey must be random. [4]Direct observation is helpful for in-depth studies of social processes, but to be useful, such observations must be made by a skilled researcher. [5]Finally, existing information can be studied as the basis for new conclusions.

____ 3. [1]Warren G. Harding was the first president elected after passage of the 19th Amendment, which gave women the right to vote. [2]_____ his presidency was rocked by scandals, some blamed women for supporting the candidate who photographed well and was considered handsome.

____ 4. [1]Throughout history, more than a few famous people were vegetarians. [2]One was Pythagoras, the famous Greek mathematician who lived in the fifth century B.C. and kept to a diet of bread, honey, and vegetables. [3]Plato and Aristotle were also vegetarians. [4]The poet Percy Bysshe Shelley became a convert to vegetarianism at twenty-one and later wrote a pamphlet in its defense. [5]_____, Count Tolstoy, the Russian author famous for *War and Peace*, not only ate no animals; he would eat no eggs.

____ 5. [1]Although not generally considered a successful president, John Quincy Adams was certainly one of our most politically active ex-presidents. [2]After failing to win reelection in 1828, he won election to the House of Representatives in 1830. [3]_____ his long tenure as congressman, he became, in the words of a Virginia congressman, "the acutest, the astutest, the archest enemy of Southern slavery that ever existed." [4]In 1841, Adams successfully argued before the Supreme Court that the Africans who had taken hold of the slave ship *Amistad*, on which they had been imprisoned, should be considered free and have the option to remain within the U.S. or return home as free people.

B. (6–9.) Fill in each blank with an appropriate transition from the box. Use each transition once.

A. during	B. following	C. immediately
D. when		

[1]In the years (6)_____ World War II, William Levitt, a brassy New York developer, led the suburban revolution. [2]Born in Brooklyn in 1907, he dropped out of New York University because "I got itchy. [3]I wanted to make a lot of money. [4]I wanted a big car and a lot of clothes." [5]He got his wish. [6]Levitt and his brother made a fortune (7)_____ the depression by building houses. [7]But the Levitts really struck it rich after the war, (8)_____ the demand for new housing skyrocketed, and they developed an efficient system of mass production. [8]In 1947, on 1,200 flat acres of Long Island farmland, they built 10,600 houses that were (9)_____ sold and inhabited by more than 40,000 people—mostly young adults under thirty-five and their children. [9]"Everyone is so young," one Levittowner noted, "that sometimes it's hard to remember how to get along with older people."

____ 10. The pattern of organization of the above selection is
    A. list of items.
    B. time order.

RELATIONSHIPS I: Test C

A. Fill in each blank with an appropriate transition from the box. Use each transition once. Then, in the space provided, write the letter of the transition you have chosen.

> A. another   B. final   C. following
> D. second   E. when

___ 1. [1]Jargon—a specialized vocabulary used by a particular group, such as lawyers, teenagers, or musicians—has several benefits for group members. [2]One benefit of jargon is that it provides a way of setting insiders apart from outsiders because only the insiders know what it means. [3]_____ benefit is that jargon strengthens the ties between insiders. [4]They use it to communicate only with each other, not with anyone else. [5]In addition, jargon is an important way for a group to maintain its identity and project a clear group image. [6]Last, jargon gives individual group members a sense of belonging, and so it raises their self-esteem.

___ 2. [1]In the nineteenth century, Europeans began adding coca to wine, tea, and lozenges. [2]_____ this trend, in 1886, an Atlanta pharmacist combined crushed coca leaves from the Andes, caffeine-rich cola nuts from West Africa, cane sugar syrup, and carbonated water in a patent medicine he called "Coca-Cola."

___ 3. [1]After observing many dying people, Elisabeth Kübler-Ross described death as an orderly transition involving five stages. [2]Typically, a person first reacts to the prospect of dying with denial. [3]The _____ phase is anger, as the person facing death sees it as a gross injustice. [4]Third, anger gives way to negotiation, as the person imagines it might be possible to avoid death by striking a bargain with God. [5]The fourth stage, resignation, often is accompanied by psychological depression. [6]Finally, a complete adjustment to death involves acceptance. [7]At this point, no longer paralyzed by fear and anxiety, the person whose life is ending sets out to make the most of whatever time remains.

___ 4. [1]Test-tube babies are the product of *in vitro* fertilization whereby doctors unite a woman's egg and a man's sperm "in glass" rather than in a woman's body. [2]_____ fertilization is successful, doctors can implant the resulting embryo in the womb of the woman who is to bear the child, or they can freeze it for use at a later time.

___ 5. [1]What causes people to join groups? [2]One reason is for security, a factor that leads people to form neighborhood-watch groups. [3]Another common reason for joining a group is a desire to be with others who share one's interests and values. [4]Some people, for instance, join computer support groups to share ideas, knowledge, and software. [5]Managers may join service groups, such as Rotary Clubs, to exchange ideas with other managers. [6]Individuals may also form groups to acquire power that is difficult if not impossible to attain alone. [7]Membership in a union or employee association, for example, provides workers with influences that they lack as individual employees. [8]Goal accomplishment is a _____ reason people join groups. [9]Mountain climbers and astronauts generally function in groups.

B. (6–9.) Fill in each blank with an appropriate transition from the box. Use each transition once.

A. another	B. for one thing	C. moreover
D. secondly		

¹Several factors influence the justice system's treatment of criminals. ²(6)_____, the sex of offenders affects the severity of sentences. ³A woman is less likely to receive the death penalty than a man. ⁴(7)_____, the court is more reluctant to send a mother to prison than a father. ⁵(8)_____ factor in the treatment of offenders is their race. ⁶Nonwhites are awarded parole and probation less often. ⁷(9)_____, blacks are executed more often for capital crimes. ⁸Finally, the age of offenders is considered in sentencing. ⁹Young offenders are given special treatment. ¹⁰And the elderly are given more lenient sentences.

____ 10. The pattern of organization of the above selection is
   A. list of items.
   B. time order.

RELATIONSHIPS I: Test D

A. (1–4.) Read the textbook passage below. Then answer the question and complete the outline that follows.

> [1]Just as factories did two centuries ago, the Information Revolution has introduced new kinds of products and new forms of communication and has changed the character of work itself. [2]In general, we see three changes. [3]One change is from tangible products to ideas. [4]The industrial era was defined by the production of goods; in the postindustrial era, work involves manipulating symbols. [5]Computer programmers, writers, financial analysts, advertising executives, architects, editors, and all sorts of consultants make up the labor force of the information age. [6]Another change is from mechanical skills to literacy skills. [7]The Industrial Revolution required mechanical skills, but the Information Revolution requires literacy skills: speaking and writing well and, of course, using computers. [8]People able to communicate effectively enjoy new opportunities; people without these skills face declining prospects. [9]A final change is that work can now be done almost anywhere. [10]Industrial technology drew workers to factories that were near power sources, but computer technology allows workers to be almost anywhere. [11]Laptop computers, cell phones, and portable fax machines can turn a home, a car, and even an airplane into a "virtual office." [12]In short, new information technology blurs the line between work and home life.

____ 1. The pattern of organization of the above selection is
   A. list of items.
   B. time order.

2–4. Complete the map of the paragraph by writing in the missing supporting details.

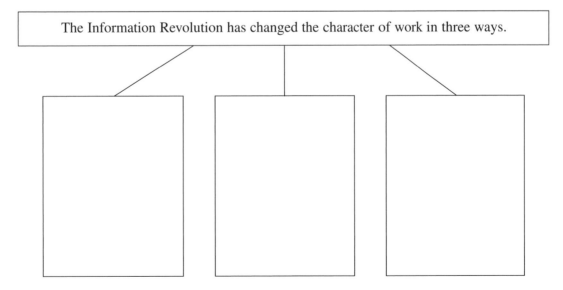

The Information Revolution has changed the character of work in three ways.

B. (5–9.) Fill in each blank with an appropriate transition from the box. Use each transition once.

A. after	B. during	C. eventually
D. first	E. until	

[1]In the early 1900s, few people understood what could be done with rockets, and financial support for rocket development was difficult to obtain. [2]It was not (5)_____ 1926 that Robert Goddard launched the (6)_____ liquid fuel rocket. [3]Despite Goddard's successes, rocket development in the United States proceeded very slowly with little government interest. [4]It was Germany that brought about the rapid development of liquid fuel rockets in the late 1930s and early 1940s. [5]The German V2 rocket, developed under the direction of Wernher von Braun (1912–1977), was the first missile to travel faster than the speed of sound, covering approximately 200 km in 5 minutes. [6]The V2 was a potent terror weapon, and thousands were launched toward Antwerp and London (7)_____ World War II. [7](8)_____ the war, the Allies carted off every bit of V2 technology they could find, including von Braun himself, who (9)_____ helped the United States put a man on the moon.

____ 10. The pattern of organization of the above selection is
     A. list of items.
     B. time order.

RELATIONSHIPS II: Test A

A. Fill in each blank with an appropriate transition from the box. Use each transition once. Then, in the space provided, write the letter of the transition you have chosen.

A. as a result	B. examples	C. for instance
D. however	E. similarly	

___ 1. [1]In early America, many men looked upon taverns as refuges where they could drink, gamble, share stories, complain about bosses, and even organize over workplace issues. [2]_____, many employers, Protestant clergymen, and female temperance reformers looked upon taverns as "the devil's playground."

___ 2. [1]In 1962 biologist Rachel Carson published *Silent Spring*, a powerful dissection of the ways that pesticides, particularly DDT, were poisoning man and nature. [2]In 1972, the federal government banned DDT, largely _____ of the outcry that Carson's book had raised.

___ 3. [1]The relative influence of a husband and wife on a particular consumer decision depends in part on the product category. [2]_____, husbands often dominate the purchase of a new automobile, while the purchase of food and home furnishings is often wife-dominated.

___ 4. [1]In Egypt, people learn to eat grasshoppers partly by watching others enjoy themselves while eating grasshoppers. [2]_____, we learn patterns of speech, styles of dress, types of energy consumption, methods of rearing children, and many other kinds of behavior by observing others.

___ 5. [1]Tacit knowledge is knowledge that is not formally or openly expressed. [2]Knowing how to win a promotion, cut through red tape, or when to reward or criticize subordinates are all _____ of tacit knowledge.

B. Label each item with the letter of its main pattern of organization.

> A. Definition and example   B. Contrast
> C. Comparison   D. Cause and effect

___ 6. [1]Why do people put themselves down regardless of what they have done? [2]People who have low self-esteem are likely to be unsure of the value of their contributions and expect others to view them negatively. [3]As a result, perhaps, people with a poor self-concept or low self-esteem find it less painful to put themselves down than to hear the criticism of others.[4]Thus, to preempt the likelihood that others will comment on their unworthiness, they do it first.

___ 7. [1]Consumers subscribe to the notion of brand personality; that is, they attribute various descriptive personality-like traits or characteristics to different brands in a wide variety of product categories. [2]For instance, consumers tend to see Volvo as representing safety, Perdue (chickens) as representing freshness, Nike as the athlete in all of us.

___ 8. [1]After years of emphasizing harshly competitive practices, companies are finding that a kinder, gentler workplace benefits the bottom line. [2]Slogans such as "greed is good" and books like *The Art of War* were prevalent in the corporate world of the 1980s and 1990s. [3]In the new millennium, however, many of the corporate success stories are related to the creation of workplaces that are open and friendly. [4]When the bosses are tyrannical and the employees are afraid to speak up, it's a recipe for disaster, such as those that happened at corporate-scandal-ridden Enron and Tyco. [5]On the other hand, when people feel free to speak their minds, it allows more creativity and productivity to emerge. [6]Employees feel they are part of a team and want to contribute. [7]It is no accident that companies that have an excellent reputation for service, such as L.L. Bean and FedEx, also foster dignity and respect in the workplace.

___ 9. [1]Heavy use of ground water causes a regional water table to drop. [2]In parts of western Texas and eastern New Mexico, the pumping of ground water from the main underground water source has caused the water table to drop 30 meters over the past few decades. [3]The lowering of the water table means that wells must be deepened and more electricity must be used to pump the water to the surface. [4]Moreover, as the water is withdrawn, the ground surface may settle because the water no longer supports the rock and sediment. [5]Mexico City has subsided more than 7 meters and portions of California's Central Valley 9 meters because of extraction of ground water. [6]Such subsidence can crack building foundations, roads, and pipelines. [7]Overpumping of ground water also causes compaction and porosity loss in rock and soil, and can permanently ruin good aquifers.

___ 10. [1]Traditionally, the American press has assumed a watchdog role, meaning that it accepts responsibility for protecting the public from deceitful, careless, incompetent, and corrupt officials. [2]In this role, the press stands ready to expose any official who violates accepted legal, ethical, and performance standards. [3]The most notable example of the watchdog role in recent decades took place during the Watergate scandal. [4]Bob Woodward and Carl Bernstein of the *Washington Post* spent months uncovering evidence that high-ranking officials in the Nixon White House were lying about their role in the burglary of the Democratic National Committee's headquarters and in their subsequent cover-up. [5]Virtually all the nation's media picked up on the *Post*'s revelations. [6]Nixon was forced to resign, as was his attorney general, John Mitchell. [7]The Watergate episode is a dramatic reminder that a vigilant press is one of society's best safeguards against abuses of political power.

RELATIONSHIPS II: Test B

A. Fill in each blank with an appropriate transition from the box. Use each transition once. Then, in the space provided, write the letter of the transition you have chosen.

> A. although   B. for instance   C. likewise
> D. on the other hand   E. so

____ 1. [1]In the nationally televised presidential debates of 1960, John F. Kennedy was tanned, confident, and dynamic, while Richard M. Nixon, recently ill, appeared drawn, haggard, and hesitant. [2]_____ radio listeners judged the contest a draw, the TV audience gave the edge to Kennedy, who shot up irreversibly in the polls.

____ 2. [1]Children of homosexuals are no more likely to be homosexual themselves than are children of heterosexuals. [2]In one study, the vast majority of adult sons of gay fathers were heterosexual. [3]_____, a study of adult children of lesbians found that a large majority identified themselves as heterosexual.

____ 3. [1]In the late 1400s, Queen Isabella of Spain decreed slavery to be illegal unless the people involved were so wicked that their conditions as slaves would be better than as free men. [2]This legal requirement probably led Spanish conquerors to exaggerate the extent of cannibalistic practices among the native peoples they encountered _____ that they could enslave them.

____ 4. [1]Lighting levels add meaning to communication messages. [2]In lecture halls and reading rooms, bright light is expected—it encourages good listening and comfortable reading. [3]_____, in a chic restaurant, a music listening room, or a television lounge, you expect the lighting to be soft and rather dim, which makes for a cozy atmosphere that invites intimate conversation.

____ 5. [1]Advertisers seek to determine an audience's characteristics. [2]The analysis of observable audience characteristics is called demographics. [3]Demographics are composed of data about a target audience's sex, age, income level, marital status, geographic location and occupation. [4]These data are observable because they are available to advertising agencies through census data and other sources. [5]Advertising agencies use demographic audience analysis to help advertisers target their messages. [6]_____, a motorcycle dealer certainly wouldn't want to advertise in a baby magazine; a candy manufacturer probably wouldn't profit from advertising in a diet and exercise magazine. [7]Advertising agencies try to match a client's product to a thoroughly defined audience so each advertising dollar is well spent.

B. Label each item with the letter of its main pattern of organization.

> A. Definition and example
> c. Comparison
> B. Contrast
> D. Cause and effect

___ 6. [1]In 1913, technological advocate Thomas Edison stated, "Books will soon be obsolete in the schools. . . . [2]It is possible to teach every branch of human knowledge with the motion picture." [3]In like manner, in the 1980s, when microcomputers became affordable, some educational visionaries predicted the end of classroom instruction and the end of the teaching profession as we know it.

___ 7. [1]An airplane is supported in flight by air passing across its wings. [2]Air traveling over the wings moves farther and faster than air traveling under the wings. [3]As a result, the air pressure is lower above the wings, and the wings experience an upward lift force. [4]This lift force decreases at low airspeeds, so most commercial jet airplanes must alter the shapes of their wings during takeoffs and landings.

___ 8. [1]The placebo effect is an apparent cure or improved state of health brought about by a substance, product, or procedure that has no generally recognized therapeutic value. [2]For instance, it is not uncommon for patients to report improvements based on what they expect, desire, or were told would happen after taking simple sugar pills that they believed were powerful drugs. [3]Although the placebo effect is generally harmless, it does account for the expenditure of millions of dollars on health products and services every year. [4]Megadoses of vitamin C have never been proven to treat cancer. [5]Mud baths do not smooth wrinkled skin, nor do electric shocks reduce muscle pain. [6]People who mistakenly use placebos when medical treatment is urgently needed increase their risk for health problems.

___ 9. [1]When students do well on a test, they tend to congratulate themselves and to attribute their success to how hard they studied, their intelligence, and so forth—all internal attributions. [2]But when a student fails a test, the external attributions fly left and right: "They were all trick questions!" [3]"I couldn't concentrate because the guy behind me kept coughing."

___ 10. [1]The fallacy of positive instances is the tendency to remember uncommon events that seem to confirm our beliefs and to forget events that disconfirm our beliefs. [2]Often, the occurrence is really nothing more than coincidence. [3]For example, you find yourself thinking of an old friend. [4]A few moments later, the phone rings and it's him. [5]You remember this seemingly telepathic event, but forget all the times that you've thought of your old friend and he did not call. [6]In other words, you remember the positive instance but fail to notice the negative instances when the anticipated event did not occur.

RELATIONSHIPS II: Test C

Read each textbook paragraph below. Then answer the questions that follow.

A. [1]For years, various sociologists have struggled to determine the causes of poverty in America. [2]One approach holds that the poor are primarily responsible for their own poverty. [3]Throughout our history, people in the United States have valued self-reliance, convinced that social standing is mostly a matter of individual talent and effort. [4]This view sees society as offering plenty of opportunity to anyone able and willing to take advantage of it. [5]From this point of view, the poor are those who cannot or will not work, women and men with fewer skills, less schooling, and little motivation. [6]An alternative position holds that society is primarily responsible for poverty. [7]Sociologists who hold this view point to the loss of jobs in our inner cities as the primary cause of poverty, claiming there is simply not enough work to support families. [8]Thus, any apparent lack of trying on the part of the poor is a result of little opportunity rather than a cause of poverty.

____ 1. The main pattern of organization of the paragraph is
   A. definition and example.   B. cause and effect.
   C. comparison.   D. contrast.

2. One transition that signals the pattern of organization of this paragraph is _____.

B. [1]Words have two kinds of meanings—denotative and connotative. [2]Denotative meaning is precise, literal, and objective. [3]It simply describes the object, person, place, idea, or event to which the word refers. [4]One way to think of a word's denotative meaning is as its dictionary definition. [5]For example, denotatively, the noun *school* means "a place, institution, or building where instruction is given." [6]Connotative meaning is more variable, figurative, and subjective. [7]Put simply, the connotative meaning is what the word suggests or implies. [8]For instance, the connotative meaning of the word *school* includes the feelings, associations, and emotions that the word touches off in different people. [9]For some people, *school* might connote personal growth, childhood friends, and a special teacher. [10]For others, it might connote frustration, discipline, and boring homework assignments.

____ 3. The main pattern of organization of the paragraph is
   A. definition and example.   B. cause and effect.
   C. comparison.   D. contrast.

4. One transition that signals the pattern of organization of this paragraph is _____.

C. [1]The biological significance of a single sperm is very different from that of a single egg. [2]For healthy men, sperm is a "renewable resource" produced by the testes throughout most of the life course. [3]A man releases hundreds of millions of sperm in a single ejaculation, technically enough to fertilize every woman in North America. [4]However, a newborn girl's ovaries contain her entire lifetime allotment of immature eggs. [5]A woman releases a single egg from the ovaries every month. [6]Whereas men are biologically capable of fathering thousands of offspring, a woman is able to bear a much smaller number of children.

____ 5. The main pattern of organization of the paragraph is
   A. definition and example.   B. cause and effect.
   C. comparison.   D. contrast.

6. One transition that signals the pattern of organization of this paragraph is _____.

D. [1]The Roman (Western) alphabet consists of twenty-six letters, each representing a different sound. [2]Chinese writing incorporates about thirty thousand pictograms, each representing a different word. [3]Just as Roman letters can be combined to produce any word, Chinese pictograms can be combined to express any idea. [4]Obviously, one advantage of the Roman system is that only a small number of symbols is required. [5]The twenty-six letters are easy to learn. [6]By contrast, the thirty thousand Chinese pictograms take a long time to learn. [7]And it is difficult to use them with a keyboard. [8]Also, when the Roman alphabet is used, only people who speak a particular language can read text written in that language. [9]On the other hand, any language can be written and read in Chinese pictograms, as long as the reader has the "key" to those pictograms. [10]In fact, speakers of many Chinese dialects who cannot understand one another's spoken language are able to communicate easily through text written in Chinese.

____ 7. The main pattern of organization of the paragraph is
   A. definition and example.   B. cause and effect.
   C. comparison.   D. contrast.

8. One transition that signals the pattern of organization of this paragraph is _____.

RELATIONSHIPS II: Test D

Read each textbook paragraph below. Then answer the questions that follow.

A. [1]Often governmental efforts to manipulate public opinion backfire when the public is made aware of the government's tactics. [2]Thus, in 1971, the United States government's attempts to build popular support for the Vietnam War were hurt when CBS News aired its documentary *The Selling of the Pentagon*, which revealed the extent and character of government efforts to sway popular sentiment. [3]In this documentary, CBS demonstrated the techniques, including planted news stories and faked film footage, that the government had used to misrepresent its activities in Vietnam. [4]These revelations, of course, had the effect of undermining public trust in all government claims.

_____ 1. The main pattern of organization of the paragraph is
    A. definition and example.   B. cause and effect.
    C. comparison.   D. contrast.

    2. One transition that signals the pattern of organization of this paragraph is _____.

B. [1]Both our 17th president, Andrew Johnson, and our 42nd president, Bill Clinton, were raised by a hard-working single mother. [2]Both were Southern Democrats. [3]Both were impeached. [4]Yet these superficial similarities in the careers of the two men mask dramatic differences between them. [5]When Andrew Johnson fired Secretary of War Stanton, he was charged with violating the Tenure of Office Act, a law that probably was unconstitutional. [6]His impeachment took place against the backdrop of a national debate over the course of post-Civil War Reconstruction, a debate that was intensely ideological. [7]In contrast, Bill Clinton was charged with lying and obstructing justice, charges that stemmed from an extramarital affair the president had conducted with a young White House intern, Monica Lewinsky. [8]Clinton's impeachment reflected the bitter partisanship and personal animosity between Democrats and Republicans in the 1990s.

_____ 3. The main pattern of organization of the paragraph is
    A. definition and example.   B. cause and effect.
    C. comparison.   D. contrast.

    4. One transition that signals the pattern of organization of this paragraph is _____.

C. [1]Almost all effective interpersonal communication requires some degree of self-disclosure. [2]The very process of making friends involves learning more about each other. [3]In the broadest sense, self-disclosure means sharing biographical data, personal ideas, and feelings. [4]Statements such as "I was 5'6" in seventh grade" reveal biographical information—facts about you as an individual. [5]Statements such as "I don't think prisons ever really rehabilitate criminals" disclose personal ideas and reveal what and how you think. [6]Statements such as "I get scared when I have to make a speech" disclose feelings. [7]Biographical disclosures are easiest to make, for they are, in a manner of speaking, a matter of public record. [8]It is statements about personal ideas and feelings that most people think of as self-disclosure.

_____ 5. The main pattern of organization of the paragraph is
A. definition and example.   B. cause and effect.
C. comparison.   D. contrast.

6. One transition that signals the pattern of organization of this paragraph is _____.

D. [1]The rubber balloon is an interesting elastic object. [2]As it's inflated with helium, the rubber balloon is stretched away from its equilibrium shape, and it exerts restoring forces that try to return it to that equilibrium shape. [3]As a result, each region of the balloon's surface experiences three forces: an inward force from the pressure of air outside, an outward force from the pressure of helium inside, and an inward force from the elastic skin of the balloon itself. [4]Since each region of surface is stationary, it must be experiencing zero net force; the outward force must balance the two inward forces. Therefore, the pressure of the helium inside the balloon must be somewhat greater than the pressure of the outside air.

_____ 7. The main pattern of organization of the paragraph is
A. definition and example.   B. cause and effect.
C. comparison.   D. contrast.

8. One transition that signals the pattern of organization of this paragraph is _____.

INFERENCES: Test A

For each item, put a check (✓) by the **two** inferences most logically based on the information provided.

1–2. "A hero is a man who does what he can."—Romain Rolland

_____ A. Heroism doesn't always consist of noticeable actions.

_____ B. Many people do not do all they can to help others.

_____ C. It is easy to be a hero.

_____ D. People don't have to be outstandingly brave to be heroic.

3–4. "The old law of 'an eye for an eye' leaves everybody blind." —Martin Luther King, Jr.

_____ A. Violence is a necessary evil.

_____ B. Responding to violence with violence leads to destruction.

_____ C. Old laws are the best laws.

_____ D. There are better ways of responding to injustice than with violence.

5–6. "Help your brother's boat across, and your own will reach the shore." —Hindu proverb

_____ A. We need each other to help us reach our goals.

_____ B. Helping someone benefits the helper as well as the receiver of help.

_____ C. People should sacrifice their well-being for the sake of others.

_____ D. Boats tend to reach shore no matter who pilots them.

7–8. The already privileged receive privileged educations. The disadvantaged receive inferior educations, and then we blame them for their failure.

_____ A. The disadvantaged fail because they do not try hard enough.

_____ B. If everyone received good educations, more people would succeed.

_____ C. Our society helps ensure that the privileged stay privileged by handicapping the disadvantaged.

_____ D. In our society, quality education is available to all, but some don't take advantage of it.

9–10. A child is not a vase to be filled, but a fire to be lit.

_____ A. Children are too wild to be able to learn very much.

_____ B. When educating children, the desires and interests of children should be addressed.

_____ C. It is easier to educate a child when the child's curiosity is aroused.

_____ D. Children must be forced to learn things.

INFERENCES: Test B

For each item, put a check (✓) by the **two** inferences most logically based on the information provided.

1–2. "I am not afraid of storms, for I am learning how to sail my ship." —Louisa May Alcott

_____ A. With education, a person can overcome obstacles.

_____ B. The speaker is an experienced sailor.

_____ C. The speaker is overconfident.

_____ D. Education can increase a person's self-confidence.

3–4. "If there is to be any peace, it will come through being, not having." —Henry Miller

_____ A. Material possessions do not bring happiness.

_____ B. It is easy to achieve peace.

_____ C. Wars are fought for material gain.

_____ D. People who continuously desire things are never at peace.

5–6. "To carry a grudge is like being stung to death by one bee." —William H. Walton

_____ A. People who carry grudges attach too much importance to something trivial.

_____ B. People are better off forgiving whoever causes them harm.

_____ C. It's less painful to carry a grudge than to be stung by a bee.

_____ D. People who carry grudges are often attacked for their beliefs.

7–8. Happy are those who dream dreams and are ready to pay the price to make them come true.

_____ A. Some dreams are not worth the price required to make them come true.

_____ B. People are happiest when they're working toward a goal.

_____ C. It's not enough to dream . . . one must take action to achieve what one wishes.

_____ D. If we wish hard enough, our dreams will come true.

9–10. An army of sheep led by a lion would defeat an army of lions led by a sheep.

_____ A. Weak leaders discourage even brave followers.

_____ B. A strong and determined person can inspire even the fearful.

_____ C. Contrary to popular belief, sheep are as brave as lions.

_____ D. Strong leadership is not all that important.

INFERENCES: Test C

A. (1–5.) Read the passage below from Rodney Dangerfield's memoir *It's Not Easy Bein' Me*. Then check the **five** statements after the passage which are most logically supported by the information given.

¹We lived in the Bronx for a year, then moved to a rooming house in Far Rockaway, Long Island, near the ocean, on July 19. ²My mother waited until that date so that she could get the place cheap—$39 for the rest of the summer. ³The three of us—my mother, my sister, and me—lived in one room, ten long blocks from the beach. ⁴But it was a beach.

⁵My first day there I saw a kid I knew from the Bronx. ⁶He was selling ice cream on the beach. ⁷That became my job for the next four summers. ⁸It was hard work for a young kid—carrying around a heavy carton of ice cream loaded with dry ice so that the ice cream wouldn't melt. ⁹It was also against the law, but no one cared—a minor offense—and I could make at least a dollar a day. ¹⁰For that kind of money I became a criminal.

¹¹That first summer I did pretty good. I saved $100, and my mother put it in a bank for me. ¹²When I looked at my bankbook a few months later, I was shocked. ¹³All my money was gone. ¹⁴When I asked my mother about this, she just said that she'd needed it. ¹⁵And that was it. ¹⁶I said to myself, *Hey, what's the big deal?* ¹⁷*It's your mother.* ¹⁸But then I thought, *She should have at least sat me down and told me what was going on before she took it.* ¹⁹That would have been easier for me, but that was how my mother did things.

_____ A. There were no laws against child labor when the author was a boy.

_____ B. The author's family was poor.

_____ C. The author used to complain a lot.

_____ D. The author's mother did not want her son to work selling ice cream.

_____ E. The author's father did not help the family.

_____ F. The author and his family probably returned to the Bronx at the end of the summer.

_____ G. The author was hurt that his mother took his money without telling him.

_____ H. The author's mother took his money to spend foolishly.

_____ I. As he grew older, the author was often in trouble with the law.

_____ J. The author's mother didn't care much about her son's feelings.

B. (6–10.) Read the passage below. Then check the **five** statements after the passage which are most logically supported by the information given.

[1]For years researchers have been studying factors that affect how long people live. [2]Money, lack of stress, a loving family, and lots of friends have all been shown to positively affect lifespan. [3]Now, researchers are finding that the one social factor which is consistently linked to longer lives in every country where it has been studied is education. [4]Researchers have arrived at this conclusion by examining the effects of changed laws on compulsory education in Sweden, Denmark, England, Wales, and the United States. [5]In every country, requiring children to spend a longer time in school led to better health. [6]For example, Dr. Adriana Lleras-Muney, an American researcher, went back and found when different states changed compulsory schooling from, say, six years to seven years. [7]Then she used census records to find out how long people lived before and after the law in each state was changed. [8]When the analysis was finished, she found that life expectancy at age 35 was extended by as much as one and a half years simply by going to school for one extra year. [9]Dr. Lleras-Muney and others point to one possible explanation—as a group, less educated people are less able to plan for the future and to delay gratification. [10]In other words, they tend to be more likely to engage in behaviors known to shorten lifespan, including smoking, drinking to excess, and engaging in dietary habits which lead to high blood pressure, diabetes, cancer, and heart disease. [11]It seems that the more education a person receives, the more willing and able he or she is to control such self-destructive habits.

_____ A. Educated people are more hopeful about the future than people with little education.

_____ B. People who drop out of high school may not know or care that smoking and drinking to excess are bad for them.

_____ C. People who have few or no friends live just as long as people with lots of friends.

_____ D. Lack of education can make a person unhappy.

_____ E. Compulsory education laws benefit society.

_____ F. There is probably no connection between education and health in countries other than the United States, Sweden, Denmark, England, and Wales.

_____ G. On average, high-school graduates tend to live longer than high-school dropouts.

_____ H. Researchers are trying to help people to live longer.

_____ I. People who drop out of high school tend to live just as long as people who graduate.

_____ J. The reasons why more education leads to better health are very clear.

INFERENCES: Test D

A. (1–5.) Read the passage below. Then check the **five** statements after the passage which are most logically supported by the information given.

[1]"In the future," the artist Andy Warhol predicted in 1968, "everybody will be world-famous for fifteen minutes." [2]Though his prediction is far from holding true today, over 40 percent of American adults nonetheless believe that they will be famous for a short time during their lives, and 30 percent regularly daydream about being famous. [3]Recently, psychologists and social scientists have been working to figure out where the desire for fame comes from, as well as precisely how (and how much) it affects people's thoughts and behavior. [4]Their research tells us that those who have an overwhelming urge to be famous are different from those merely seeking wealth and power, in that the drive for fame is born out of a need not just for personal comfort, but for social acceptance. [5]This need for acceptance may stem from childhood experiences of rejection or neglect, and may grow stronger in aging individuals who feel their lives are passing them by without bringing them the fame they crave. [6]Accordingly, studies show that people who are extra sensitive to the notion of their own mortality are also more likely than others to become fame-seekers. [7]The knowledge that we'll be remembered by the world, psychologists suggest, can provide great comfort in the face of our own death. [8]Since so few of us can actually be famous in reality, however, the drive for fame tends to cause much more psychological discomfort for fame-seekers than it does relief. [9]Moreover, those who do become famous often find the self-consciousness that fame brings with it to be much more tormenting than the drive to become famous in the first place. [10]Overall, studies conclude, people are generally happier and more fulfilled when they center their lives not around fame, but around self-acceptance and friendship. [11]So what's all the fuss about fifteen minutes?

_____ A. People who were neglected as children tend to seek attention as adults.

_____ B. Those who seek fame usually attain it.

_____ C. Having a few good friends can be just as satisfying as being famous, if not more so.

_____ D. People who are famous sometimes have a hard time coping with the constant attention that fame brings.

_____ E. To become famous is the surest way to become truly happy.

_____ F. All people desire fame.

_____ G. People who seek fame often lack self-esteem.

_____ H. The author believes that fame-seekers are generally wasting their time.

_____ I. People who seek fame usually derive great satisfaction when they finally attain it.

_____ J. People who are famous are generally happier than people who are not.

B. (6–10.) Read the passage below. Then check the **five** statements after the passage which are most logically supported by the information given.

[1]In 1892 Philip G. Hubert Jr., writing for *Century Magazine*, proposed an elaborate but entirely impractical scheme for extending vacations to members of the working class. [2]He suggested that poor tenement dwellers "give up their few rooms, store their goods at small expense," and thereby "save enough on the rent to pay for their food during the weeks away." [3]Families could move to the south shore of Long Island or into New Jersey, where they could pitch tents and live more healthfully and just as cheaply. [4]Hubert estimated that even the "typical family of slop-shop clothing makers," including two working parents and four children, could camp out for ten weeks "at an average weekly expense of not more than $5." [5]He did admit some disadvantages to his proposal: "There would be rainy days and the various unpleasant features and hardships of camping out. [6]There would be no corner liquor-store for the men, nor corner gossip for the women. [7]The daily toil might even be a trifle harder, owing to lack of conveniences. [8]Meat would be difficult to get and to keep." [9]Still, the advantages, he felt, would far outweigh such minor liabilities.

_____ A. Hubert's scheme was never put into practice.

_____ B. In 1892, the working class did not get paid vacations.

_____ C. Members of the working class often owned their own homes in 1892.

_____ D. Hubert believed that working-class people liked to drink and gossip.

_____ E. If given the chance, working-class families would have gladly done as Hubert suggested.

_____ F. In the 1890s, the south shore of Long Island and most of New Jersey were very crowded.

_____ G. In the 1890s, working-class families generally had only one breadwinner.

_____ H. Hubert believed that living outdoors was healthier than living indoors.

_____ I. Hubert was not a member of the working class.

_____ J. Hubert respected the work that the clothing makers performed.

PURPOSE AND TONE: Test A

A. In the space provided, indicate whether the primary purpose of each sentence is to inform (**I**), to persuade (**P**), or to entertain (**E**).

_____ 1. Chimpanzees, gorillas, and elephants are among the few animals who can recognize themselves in mirrors.

_____ 2. This duck walks into a drugstore and he says, "Gimme some Chapstick and put it on my bill."

_____ 3. Parents should carefully monitor their children's use of the Internet.

_____ 4. I never knew what real happiness was until I got married—then it was too late.

_____ 5. Because of their brilliant direction, great acting, and powerful insights into the nature of American life, the *Godfather I* and *II* movies should be considered among the best American movies of the past fifty years.

_____ 6. About 65 million years ago, the last dinosaurs vanished in a mass extinction which coincided with a direct hit by an asteroid the size of Mount Everest.

B. Each of the following passages illustrates one of the tones named in the box below. In each space provided, write the letter of the tone that applies to the passage. Two tone choices will be left over.

A. informal and affectionate	B. objective	C. praising and appreciative
D. regretful	E. scornful	F. tolerant and compassionate

_____ 7. [1]I played football through grade school, co-captained my high-school team, and went on to become an inside linebacker and defensive captain at the NCAA Division 1 level. [2]I learned to be an animal. [3]Coaches took notice of animals. [4]Animals made first team. [5]Being an animal meant being fanatically aggressive and ruthlessly competitive. [6]If I saw an arm in front of me, I trampled it. [7]Whenever blood was spilled, I nodded approval. [8]Broken bones (not mine, of course) were secretly seen as little victories within the bigger struggle. [9]The coaches taught me to "punish the other man," but little did I suspect that I was devastating my own body at the same time. [10]There were broken noses, ribs, fingers, toes and teeth, torn muscles and ligaments, bruises, bad knees, and busted lips, and the gradual pulverizing of my spinal column that, by the time my jock career was long over at age 30, had resulted in seven years of near-constant pain. [11]It was a long road to the surgeon's office.

_____ 8. [1]Teachers usually have no way of knowing that they have made a difference in a child's life, even when they have made a dramatic one. [2]But for children who are used to thinking of themselves as stupid or not worth talking to or deserving rape and beatings, a good teacher can provide an astonishing revelation. [3]A good teacher can give a child at least a chance to think, "*She* thinks I'm worth something. [4]Maybe I am." [5]Good teachers create new directions in the rivers of children passing by, and over the years they alter hundreds of lives. [6]Many people find it easy to imagine unseen webs of malevolent conspiracy in the world, and they are not always wrong. [7]But there is also an innocence that conspires to hold humanity together, and it is made of people who can never fully know the good that they have done.

_____ 9. ¹The McDonaldization of society—the standardization of everyday life—does not refer just to the robotlike assembly of food. ²As sociologist George Ritzer points out, this process is occurring throughout society—and it is transforming our lives. ³Want to do some shopping? ⁴Shopping malls offer one-stop shopping in safely controlled environments. ⁵Planning a trip? ⁶Travel agencies offer "package" tours. ⁷They will transport middle-class Americans to ten European capitals in fourteen days. ⁸All visitors experience the same hotels, restaurants, and other scheduled sites—and no one need fear meeting a real "native" and having an authentic experience in another culture. ⁹Want to keep up with events? ¹⁰*USA Today* spews out McNews—short, bland, unanalytical pieces that require little if any thinking and can be digested between gulps of the McShake or the McBurger.

_____ 10. ¹Just as infants seem to be biologically programmed to learn language, parents seem to be biologically programmed to encourage language development by the way they speak to infants and toddlers. ²People in every culture, especially parents, use a style of speech called *motherese*, or infant-directed speech, with babies. ³Motherese is characterized by very distinct pronunciation, a simplified vocabulary, short sentences, high pitch, and exaggerated intonation and expression. ⁴Content is restricted to topics that are familiar to the child, and "baby talk" is often used—simplified words such as "go bye-bye" and "night-night." ⁵Questions are often asked, encouraging a response from the infant. ⁶Research by psychologist Ann Fernald has shown that infants prefer infant-directed speech to language spoken in an adult conversational style.

PURPOSE AND TONE: Test B

Ten quotations in the story below are preceded by a blank space. Identify the tone of each italicized quotation by writing in the letter of one of these tones.

A. blunt	B. enthusiastic	C. helpful
D. indignant	E. insolent	F. persuasive
G. pleading	H. pompous	I. regretful
J. startled		

As I was relaxing at home the other evening, the phone rang.

_____ 1. *"Hi!"* said the very young-sounding woman on the phone. *"I have some really exciting news for you! You have won a COMPLETELY FREE weekend at The Grande, the finest hotel in Atlantic City! Isn't that wonderful?"*

I knew from experience that "free" meant that I would be expected to sit through a long, high-pressure presentation from someone trying to sell me something, probably a time-share vacation plan.

_____ 2. *"No, thanks,"* I told the young woman. *"I'm not interested."*

_____ 3. *"Oh, but sir!"* she quickly said. *"I don't think you understand! This is a completely free weekend at one of Atlantic City's most beautiful hotels! You'll enjoy it very much."*

"Thank you, but no," I repeated.

_____ 4. Her voice changed remarkably. *"What are you, some kind of millionaire?"* she snapped. *"You like to pay for things?"*

_____ 5. My jaw dropped. *"You are a very rude young woman!"* I exclaimed. *"Let me speak to your manager."*

I thought she would hang up on me. But to my surprise, she put me through to her supervisor, who sounded as young as she did.

_____ 6. I repeated our conversation, adding, *"Maybe it would be a good idea to provide some training in customer relations."*

"I'm so sorry that happened to you, sir," said the young man. "She'll be fired immediately."

"What?" I said. "No! Wait! I don't want her fired. Couldn't you just talk to her about it?"

_____ 7. _"There is absolutely no excuse for how she spoke to you, sir,"_ he continued. He sounded more self-important every moment. _"I simply won't put up with such behavior among my employees."_

_____ 8. _"I really think you're overreacting,"_ I said. _"Please, I know that telemarketing must be a really hard way to make a living. She wasn't that bad. She was probably just having a bad day. I don't want to get her fired. Really, let's just forget it."_

I hung up. My wife came into the kitchen in time to see me leaning back in my chair, staring up at the ceiling in despair.

_____ 9. _"What in the world is the matter?"_ she asked.

_____ 10. _"I think I just got some poor woman fired from her job,"_ I said. _"I feel terrible."_

PURPOSE AND TONE: Test C

Read each of the selections below. Then carefully consider the questions that follow, and write the letters of the best responses.

A. [1]In 2000, John Welch of General Electric paid himself $144 million, while also receiving millions of dollars' worth of perks, such as a company-paid home and a private box in the stadium where the Boston Red Sox play. [2]When Welch left General Electric in 2001, the firm granted him a pension of $9 million annually, plus lifetime use of a corporate jet, an extravagant Manhattan apartment, and such absurd extras as permission to send his liquor bills to the company. [3]Hundreds of average General Electric employees were laid off—some of their lives ruined—to fund Welch's carnival of greed. [4]And greed it was in every sense, since Welch avidly grabbed from others but gave almost nothing away. [5]Papers filed by Welch himself in a divorce proceeding declared that he had a net worth of $456 million but donated a mere $3 million annually to charity. [6]This is a miser's sum, since $456 million conservatively invested would yield around $20 million annually, allowing Welch to give away much more while still living in opulence and not touching his principal.

_____ 1. The purpose of this paragraph is to
   A. inform readers of the benefits of being a CEO.
   B. persuade readers that former CEO John Welch is greedy.
   C. entertain readers with a story of the extravagant lifestyle of a millionaire CEO.

_____ 2. The tone of the paragraph can be described as
   A. critical but understanding.
   B. distressed but optimistic.
   C. outraged and scornful.

B. [1]If you continue to eat bad food, you'll continue to suffer bad health. [2]If you want things to change, remember that change starts with you. [3]Your own life, your own family. [4]Get aware. [5]Get active. [6]Parents, you are your children's primary role models. [7]What they see you do, they'll imitate. [8]Take charge of your kids' diets, their attitudes about food, their daily physical activity, their schools. [9]Make the buying, preparing and enjoying of good, wholesome food a cherished family activity again. [10]You don't have to completely stop eating burgers and fries—I know I haven't—but you can stop buying them processed and chemically infused from fast-food joints, and patronize a real sandwich shop that makes you a real burger and real fries right there when you order. [11]Stop driving yourself and your kids everywhere from door to door. [12]Get out and walk or ride a bike with them. [13]Plant some veggies with them in your backyard. [14]I promise you'll remember how fun it is and how good it makes you feel. [15]And you'll be teaching your kids invaluable life habits.

_____ 3. The primary purpose of this paragraph is to
   A. inform readers that a diet of fast food is not healthy.
   B. persuade readers to change their eating habits for the better.
   C. entertain readers with stories of mouthwatering meals.

_____ 4. The tone of the paragraph can be described as
   A. straightforward and encouraging.
   B. outspoken but ambivalent.
   C. bitter and cynical.
   D. informal and humorous.

C. ¹What's the secret of a happy marriage? ²Call me a romantic if you want, but for me, the answer is the same simple, beautiful idea that has been making relationships work for thousands of years: separate bathrooms. ³You give two people room to spread out their toiletry articles, and you have the basis of a long-term relationship. ⁴But you make them perform their personal hygiene activities in the same small enclosed space, year in and year out, constantly finding the other person's bodily hairs stuck on their deodorant sticks, and I don't care how loving they were when they started out. ⁵I don't care if they were Romeo and Juliet. ⁶They'll be slipping poison into each other's non-dairy creamer.

_____ 5. The primary purpose of this paragraph is to
   A. inform.
   B. persuade.
   C. entertain.

PURPOSE AND TONE: Test D

Read each of the selections below. Then carefully consider the questions that follow and write the letters of the best responses.

A. [1]Antibiotics should be prescribed with restraint and care. [2]Why? [3]Besides performing their intended function, they commonly disrupt the balances among bacterial populations that normally compete for resources in the mammalian intestines and of yeast cells in the vaginal canal. [4]Such disruptions lead to secondary infections. [5]Worse yet, antibiotics have been overprescribed in the human population. [6]Too frequently they have been used for simple infections that many individuals could have overcome successfully on their own. [7]Disturbingly, antibiotics have lost their punch. [8]Over time, they did destroy the most susceptible cells of target populations. [9]But they also favored their replacement by much more resistant cells. [10]Millions of people around the world are now dying each year of tuberculosis, cholera, and other bacterial infections. [11]Even vancomycin, held in reserve as "the antibiotic of last resort," is no longer effective against certain pathogenic strains of bacteria. [12]In 1996, the World Health Organization announced that, in the race for supremacy, pathogens are sprinting ahead.

_____ 1. The primary purpose of this paragraph is to
    A. inform readers about antibiotics in the world today.
    B. persuade readers that antibiotics should be prescribed less often than they currently are.
    C. entertain readers with exciting stories of medical breakthroughs.

_____ 2. The tone of this paragraph can be described as
    A. indignant and determined.
    B. concerned and straightforward.
    C. calming and tolerant.
    D. optimistic and encouraging.

B. [1]We pulled out into traffic and immediately were serenaded by a blaring horn from a car speeding by us in the next lane. [2]Apparently we had pulled out in front of the car, causing the driver to swerve quickly to avoid hitting us. [3]We felt bad and were thankful that nothing serious had happened, but the other driver wasn't so quick to forgive. [4]For several miles she maneuvered to make us pull over, or slowed down in the neighboring lane in order to pull alongside our car. [5]I wanted nothing to do with this and slowed down as well to avoid facing her. [6]Finally, she pulled over as she approached a right-hand turn, and as we went by, she stuck her head out the window and screamed venomous slurs our way. [7]I'll never forget the expression on the woman's face as we went by. [8]It was filled with such hatred, such rage.

_____ 3. The primary purpose of this paragraph is to
    A. inform us of how easily auto accidents can happen.
    B. persuade us that road rage is an increasingly common phenomenon.
    C. entertain us with a vivid and scary account of a frightening incident.

_____ 4. The author's tone is
    A. revengeful and critical.
    B. depressed and pessimistic.
    C. embarrassed and shocked.

C. [1]The right to say what we want, where we want, is the cornerstone of a free society, and, as such, is near and dear to Americans. [2]Justice William O. Douglas stated, "Restriction of free thought and free speech is the most dangerous of all subversions. [3]It is the one un-American act that could most easily defeat us." [4]Despite our courts' vigilant protection of this right, however, it is not an absolute right. [5]The great Supreme Court justice Oliver Wendell Holmes wrote that freedom of speech does not give the person a right to yell "Fire!" in a crowded theater or to knowingly and maliciously say or write lies that damage the reputation of another. [6]In schools, freedom of expression must be balanced with the school's responsibility to maintain a safe and orderly environment and to protect people's feelings and reputations.

___ 5. The primary purpose of this paragraph is to
   A. inform us of the evolution of the concept of free speech.
   B. persuade us of the importance and true nature of free speech.
   C. entertain us with famous quotations spoken by Supreme Court justices.

ARGUMENT: Test A

A. (1–4.) In each group, one statement is the point of an argument, and the other statements are support for that point. In the space provided, write the letter of the point of each group.

___ *Group 1*

    A. When angry, a Navajo Indian will most likely speak extra quietly.
    B. Japanese people tend to laugh when they are embarrassed.
    C. Displays of emotion and their meanings vary greatly from culture to culture.
    D. A native of the Andaman Islands will sit in a visitor's lap and cry in order to show happiness.

___ *Group 2*

    A. Irrigation made ranching and homesteading possible in areas where water was scarce.
    B. Although the Winchester rifle or Colt revolver was often credited with "winning the West," there were actually far less glamorous factors which contributed to Western settlement.
    C. Barbed wire enabled cattle ranchers to raise huge herds on ample grazing land without worrying about them wandering off.
    D. The railroad brought settlers, supplies, jobs, and mail, and made the concept of a single, undivided, universally accessible America a reality.

___ *Group 3*

    A. The Pima Indians of the American Southwest are particularly prone to diabetes.
    B. Sickle-cell anemia is far more common among black people than among people of other races.
    C. A serious disease called Tay-Sachs affects people of Eastern European Jewish descent.
    D. Certain genetic or genetically influenced diseases are more common within specific ethnic groups.

___ *Group 4*

    A. In the 19th century, theatergoers often felt free to "participate" in the performance.
    B. It was common for audiences to join in famous speeches and familiar songs.
    C. When audiences particularly enjoyed a song, speech, or scene, they cried aloud, stamped their feet, and often stopped the show to demand an encore.
    D. To express disapproval, 19th century audiences hissed, jeered, and even threw things at the performers.

B. Read the three items of support (the evidence) in the group below. Then, in the space provided, write the letter of the point that is adequately supported by that evidence.

Support:

> • Noah Webster's *American Spelling Book*, which was published in 1783, became the most widely used schoolbook during the early nineteenth century.
> • Webster's *American Dictionary of the English Language* (1828) contained the first-time appearance of such American words as *plantation, hickory, presidential,* and *pecan.*
> • Noah Webster campaigned for free schools for both boys and girls in which children could learn the virtues of liberty, hard work, and morality.

_____ 5. Which **point** is adequately supported by all the evidence above?
    A. Early Americans considered education to be vitally important to the growth of the country.
    B. Known as the "schoolmaster of the republic," Noah Webster helped create a sense of American language and national culture.
    C. Noah Webster maintained that American culture was fundamentally different from the culture of England.
    D. Noah Webster was America's first educational reformer.

ARGUMENT: Test B

A. (1–3.) In each group, one statement is the point of an argument, and the other statements are support for that point. In the space provided, write the letter of the point of each group.

___ *Group 1*

  A. Physicians now help people deal with baldness, wrinkles, small breasts, and sleeplessness.
  B. Problems that used to be accepted as part of life are now considered matters for medical attention.
  C. Some criminologists have defined antisocial behavior as a medical problem.
  D. Some men take prescription drugs in order to increase their sexual potency.

___ *Group 2*

  A. Allicin, the same substance that gives garlic its odor, kills bacteria, viruses, and funguses.
  B. Garlic has been shown to lower blood pressure.
  C. Modern scientists have found that eating garlic really does have valuable health benefits.
  D. Cloves of garlic contain selenium, a nutrient that helps prevent the oxidation in cells which can lead to cancer.

___ *Group 3*

  A. Some believe that Jack the Ripper was a Russian doctor named Alexander Pedachenko, who had already murdered a streetwalker in Paris.
  B. There are differing opinions on just who really was Jack the Ripper, the person who murdered prostitutes by grabbing them from behind and slitting their throats.
  C. One investigator thinks that Jack the Ripper may have been a Jill—an insane woman who roamed the streets.
  D. One popular mystery writer recently concluded that Jack the Ripper was actually a famous Victorian artist named Walter Sickert.

B. Read the three items of support (the evidence) in each group below. Then, in the space provided, write the letter of the point that is adequately supported by that evidence.

Support:

> - Many Poles found work in the vast steel plants of Pittsburgh, and Russian Jews often went into the garment industry and street-peddling trade in New York City.
> - California fruit orchards and vegetable farms employed numerous Japanese immigrants.
> - In Boston and New York City, second-generation Irish took advantage of their prominent place in the Democratic party to become public school teachers, firefighters, and police officers.

____ 4. Which **point** is adequately supported by all the evidence above?
   A. In the late 1800s and early 1900s, most immigrants to America were assured of finding jobs.
   B. In the late 1800s and early 1900s, specific groups of immigrants often gravitated toward particular kinds of jobs.
   C. In the late 1800s and early 1900s, specific groups of immigrants gravitated toward major cities, where they knew they could find work.
   D. In the late 1800s and early 1900s, many native-born Americans feared losing their jobs to immigrants of various nationalities.

Support:

> - Magic was a technical subject that combined expertise in the properties of plants and animals with theories about the composition of human and heavenly bodies.
> - Magic had its own language, a mixture of ancient words and sounds with significant numbers and catchphrases.
> - Magicians specialized: some concentrated on herbs and plants, others on the diseases of the body.

____ 5. Which **point** is adequately supported by all the evidence above?
   A. In some respects, magic in the Middle Ages operated in much the same way as science does today.
   B. In the Middle Ages, magicians were just as effective as modern doctors.
   C. In the Middle Ages, a knowledge of magic was passed on from generation to generation.
   D. In the Middle Ages, magic could be used for good or evil.

ARGUMENT: Test C

A. (1–2.) In each group, one statement is the point of an argument, and the other statements are support for that point. In the space provided, write the letter of the point of each group.

___ *Group 1*

    A. In Hawaii, Madame Pele is regarded as a goddess who controls volcanic eruptions.

    B. In Iceland, Loki, of Norse mythology, is thought to be imprisoned underground, blowing steam and lava up through fissures.

    C. Pacific Northwest Indians saw the Cascade volcanoes as warrior gods who would sometimes throw red-hot boulders at each other.

    D. Not surprisingly, myths and religions relating gods to volcanoes flourish in cultures that live with volcanoes.

___ *Group 2*

    A. The first settlers of Virginia were usually single men in their twenties, while New England was settled by families.

    B. There were major differences between the New England colonies and the southern colonies of Maryland and Virginia.

    C. The settlers of Virginia and Maryland came looking for adventure and opportunity, while New England settlers came seeking religious freedom.

    D. The economy of colonial Virginia revolved around one crop—tobacco—while New England developed a more varied economy.

B. Each point is followed by three statements that provide relevant support and three that do not. In the spaces, write the letters of the **three** relevant statements of support.

Point: In ancient Rome, the paterfamilias (father and head of household) was the absolute master of his home and family.

    A. Some Roman slaves lived and worked alongside the free members of the family, and worshiped the family gods.

    B. Roman wives played an informal role in the moral education of their children.

    C. Only at the father's death did his sons, even if long grown and married, achieve legal and financial independence.

    D. If there were too many mouths to feed or the child was simply unwanted, the father could command that the infant be killed or abandoned.

    E. If he desired, the father could sell the free members of his family into slavery.

    F. Roman families without heirs could adopt children.

    3–5. *Items that logically support the point:*   _____   _____   _____

Point: Today's workers are becoming more and more closely monitored.

A. Office supervisors know precisely how long each worker takes for each telephone call.

B. Many employees are able to work from home these days due to the ease of communicating via computer.

C. Surveillance cameras mounted in the workplace allow bosses in remote locations to peer over the shoulders of workers.

D. Increasingly, temporary workers are taking the place of fulltime employees.

E. Computers became a common feature of many offices in the late 1970s and early 1980s.

F. With specialized software, bosses can examine everything employees read online, everything they write, and every Web site they visit.

6–8. *Items that logically support the point:* _____ _____ _____

ARGUMENT: Test D

A. In the following group, one statement is the point of an argument, and the other statements are support for that point. In the space provided, write the letter of the point of this group.

___ *Group 1*

    A. In traditional Japanese theater, salt was sprinkled on the stage before each performance to protect the actors from evil spirits.

    B. In Haiti, the only way to break a spell and bring a zombie back to life is with salt.

    C. The British for centuries carried salt to a new home in order to ensure favorable circumstances for the people who lived there.

    D. The idea that salt has protective properties appears in diverse cultures.

B. Read the three items of support (the evidence) in each group below. Then, in the space provided, write the letter of the point that is adequately supported by that evidence.

Support:

> - An ongoing lawsuit alleges that many children have suffered obesity, diabetes, heart disease, high blood pressure, elevated cholesterol, and related health problems after being misled by fast-food restaurant chains about the health-related aspects of their food.
> - Stockholders have filed suit against companies from Audible, Inc., to AstraZeneca PLC claiming that they had received inadequate information about the value of those stocks at the time of purchase.
> - McDonald's lost a legendary case alleging a failure to inform customers about their unexpectedly hot coffee, which is served at a temperature about 20 degrees higher than that of coffee served at other restaurants.

___ 2. Which **point** is adequately supported by all the evidence above?

    A. Lawsuits against major corporations have increased tremendously in the past few years.

    B. Americans have been known to file suit against companies based upon misleading or missing information.

    C. Americans who file suit against major corporations stand a good chance of winning.

    D. Fast-food companies such as McDonalds are the corporations that are most likely to be sued by U.S. consumers.

C. The point below is followed by three statements that provide relevant support and three that do not. In the spaces, write the letters of the **three** relevant statements of support.

Point: When the Black Death struck Europe in the 1300s, people tried to explain its cause in various ways.

   A. Preachers saw the plague as divine punishment for sin.

   B. Across Europe, terrified people thought that by joining penitential groups that prayed, fasted, and even whipped themselves, they could turn away divine wrath through self-mortification.

   C. Ordinary people frequently accused Jews of causing it by poisoning drinking water.

   D. The Black Death was carried by the fleas of infected rats.

   E. The last outbreak of the Black Death in Europe was the 1771 epidemic in Moscow that killed 60,000.

   F. The medical faculty of Paris announced that the plague was the result of the conjunction of the planets Saturn, Jupiter, and Mars, which caused a corruption of the surrounding air.

3–5.   *Items that logically support the point:*   _____   _____   _____

CRITICAL READING: Test A (Fact and Opinion)

Identify facts with an **F**, opinions with an **O**, and the **one** combination of fact and opinion with an **F+O**.

_____ 1. The average American creates 4.5 pounds of garbage daily.

_____ 2. As an incentive to reduce solid waste, Americans should be charged for trash pick-up based upon the amount of garbage they generate.

_____ 3. Notre Dame's Knute Rockne was the greatest college football coach of all time.

_____ 4. The first college football game was played between teams from Princeton and Rutgers Universities on November 6, 1869.

_____ 5. In 1962, President John F. Kennedy set a goal for the United States of landing a man on the moon and bringing him back alive before the end of the decade.

_____ 6. It's a shame that billions of dollars are being spent on manned spaceflights while there are so many problems on Earth that need to be addressed.

_____ 7. People who insist on purchasing purebred dogs and cats when there are so many mixed-breed animals available for adoption are being selfish.

_____ 8. There are currently over 800 breeds of dogs and 35 to 70 breeds of cats.

_____ 9. Ernest Hemingway was famous as a rugged outdoorsman as well as a writer.

_____ 10. Ernest Hemingway was wrong to write favorably about bullfighting, since killing bulls for sport is cruel.

_____ 11. Ernest Hemingway, who won the Nobel Prize for Literature in 1954, was the greatest American writer of the 20th century.

_____ 12. In 2006, billionaire Warren Buffet announced that he planned to give away most of his fortune to charity.

_____ 13. Rich people must follow the lead of Warren Buffet and donate a large portion of their fortunes to charity.

_____ 14. The term "marriage" should apply only to heterosexual unions.

_____ 15. In recent years, many gay and lesbian couples have sought the right to marry.

_____ 16. The March 2003 invasion of Iraq was the worst foreign policy blunder in American history.

_____ 17. In March 2003, the United States invaded Iraq and toppled the regime of Saddam Hussein.

_____ 18. People would be better off if they reduced their consumption of coffee and other caffeinated beverages.

_____ 19. Coffee is the second most traded commodity in the world.

_____ 20. Ritalin is a drug which has been prescribed to children to help focus their attention if they are hyperactive and cannot concentrate.

CRITICAL READING: Test B (Propaganda Techniques)

A. Each pair of items below illustrates a particular propaganda technique. On the line next to each item, write the letter of the main technique being used.

_____ 1. • A very pretty, wholesome-looking young woman wraps herself in a robe that has been washed in a particular brand of laundry detergent.

   • A hospital chain uses a portrait of Benjamin Franklin in its advertisements and claims that it, like Franklin, stands for innovation.

    A. Name calling   C. Glittering generalities
    B. Testimonial   D. Transfer

_____ 2. • "Cleans like magic," states an ad for a household cleaning product.

   • In an ad for hair dye, a model proclaims that "It's not just hair color, it's color that works for me."

    A. Name calling   C. Glittering generalities
    B. Testimonial   D. Plain folks

_____ 3. • A famous basketball player advises us to drink a particular brand of sports drink.

   • A world champion cyclist and cancer survivor appears in an ad for a manufacturer of anti-cancer medications.

    A. Transfer   C. Bandwagon
    B. Testimonial   D. Name calling

_____ 4. • The fast food industry labels critics of their industry as "food police," "cookie cops," and "the grease Gestapo."

   • A candidate for Congress calls his opponent a "limousine liberal" who would leave the country open to terrorist attack.

    A. Transfer   C. Plain folks
    B. Bandwagon   D. Name calling

_____ 5. • A cable company claims that more and more people are switching to it to access the Internet.

   • A TV commercial for a brand of soft drink shows people from all walks of life refreshing themselves by drinking the soft drink.

    A. Transfer   C. Bandwagon
    B. Plain folks   D. Name calling

_____ 6. • An average-looking, casually dressed American family enjoys tacos flavored with a particular brand of taco seasoning.

   • A balding, middle-aged man and his wife watch in satisfaction as a liquid drain opener unclogs their kitchen sink.

    A. Transfer   C. Testimonial
    B. Plain folks   D. Name calling

B. Below are descriptions of four actual ads. On each line, write the letter of the main propaganda technique that applies to the ad.

    A. Bandwagon   D. Plain folks
    B. Testimonial   E. Name calling
    C. Transfer   F. Glittering generalities

_____ 7. An ad for the *Wall Street Journal* features men wearing hard hats on a construction site, reading the paper on their lunch break.

_____ 8. An ad for a medication which boosts the immune system of those undergoing chemotherapy features an attractive older woman painting at an easel. The woman says, "I'm ready to take on chemo. And then, take on my next canvas."

_____ 9. An ad for Orbitz travel service features snapshots of a number of children and their parents enjoying vacations. The text announces, "More for the kid in all of us."

_____ 10. Business entrepreneur and pro basketball team owner Mark Cuban claims to "enjoy every minute" of using a particular brand of hand-held digital device.

CRITICAL READING: Test C (Errors in Reasoning)

A. Each pair of items below illustrates a particular error in reasoning. On the line next to each item, write the letter of the logical fallacy contained in both items. Choose from the three fallacies shown in the box below.

> **A** Circular reasoning *(a statement repeats itself rather than providing a real supporting reason to back up an argument)*
> **B** Personal attack *(ignores the issue under discussion and concentrates instead on the character of the opponent)*
> **C** Straw man *(an argument is made by claiming an opponent holds an extreme position and then opposing that extreme position)*

_____ 1. • Terrence just purchased a German-made sports car. He must not care that he's helping to lay off American auto workers.

 • Congressman Whittaker opposes the death penalty. It must not bother him if murderers are set free to prey upon innocent people.

_____ 2. • Bonnie is always talking about people behind their backs because she's an incurable gossip.

 • My algebra instructor should be fired because she's a terrible teacher.

_____ 3. • It's amazing that Jennifer Stiler has the nerve to run for mayor. Do people forget that when she was a teenager, she had a child out of wedlock?

 • My opponent for Congress is a decorated Vietnam War veteran—but the injury he received was due to his own negligence.

_____ 4. • Karl watches football all Sunday afternoon and evening because he's a die-hard football fan.

 • Reese Witherspoon is the perfect actress to play that part because she's really talented.

_____ 5. • Senator Treadwell has come out in favor of civil unions for gays. Evidently he doesn't care if gays pressure our kids to adopt their sinful lifestyle.

 • Joan has joined a group that opposes construction of a new baseball stadium in our neighborhood. I guess she wants to see our pro baseball team leave town.

B. In the space provided, write the letter of the fallacy contained in each pair of arguments. Choose from the three fallacies shown in the box below.

> **A** False cause *(the argument assumes that the order of events alone shows cause and effect)*
>
> **B** False comparison *(the argument assumes that two things being compared are more alike than they really are)*
>
> **C** Either-or *(the argument assumes that there are only two sides to a question)*

_____ 6. • Andy only got me a small box of chocolates for Valentine's Day. That must mean he doesn't really care for me.

• If you don't study at least three hours a night, you're not serious about going to college.

_____ 7. • When I was a girl, the teacher's word was law, so I don't know where kids today get the idea that they can question authority.

• My parents stayed together for forty-seven years, so I don't see why we need to go to a marriage counselor.

_____ 8. • The last time I shopped at the mall, my wallet was stolen. They have poor security there.

• Soon after the president took office, the economy slowed down. He must not know what he's doing.

_____ 9. • I was always a star student, so I know my kids will be college-bound.

• Fifty years ago we didn't have all these expensive medical tests, and people got along just fine without them.

_____ 10. • Excerpt from a chain letter: "If you send this letter to five other people, something wonderful will happen to you."

• Yesterday I forgot to take vitamin C, and this morning I woke up with a cold. Now I know that vitamin C actually does prevent colds.

CRITICAL READING: Test D

A. Identify each fact with an **F** and each opinion with an **O**.

_____ 1. In the United States, the birth rate has declined steadily over the past decade.

_____ 2. It is immoral for couples to have children with the aid of a surrogate mother.

_____ 3. The typical American consumes three burgers and four orders of fries every week.

B. On the line next to each item, write the letter of the propaganda technique being used.

_____ 4. An ad for a luxury car encourages us to "reach higher."

    A. Name calling   C. Glittering generalities
    B. Testimonial   D. Transfer

_____ 5. A pretty young woman mischievously splashes water on the bare chest of a handsome young man in an ad for a cruise line.

    A. Plain folks   C. Glittering generalities
    B. Testimonial   D. Transfer

_____ 6. A candidate for Congress states that his opponent has a "dirty little secret."

    A. Name calling   C. Bandwagon
    B. Testimonial   D. Transfer

_____ 7. A Grammy-winning musician endorses a line of high-end audio equipment.

    A. Name calling   C. Glittering generalities
    B. Testimonial   D. Transfer

C. In the space provided, write the letter of the fallacy contained in the argument. Choose from the six fallacies shown in the box below.

A	Circular reasoning *(a statement repeats itself rather than providing a real supporting reason to back up an argument)*
B	Personal attack *(ignores the issue under discussion and concentrates instead on the character of the opponent)*
C	Straw man *(an argument is made by claiming an opponent holds an extreme position and then opposing that extreme position)*
D	False cause *(the argument assumes that the order of events alone shows cause and effect)*
E	False comparison *(the argument assumes that two things being compared are more alike than they really are)*
F	Either-or *(the argument assumes that there are only two sides to a question)*

_____ 8. The crime rate started going up about the same time that they took prayer out of public schools. If they reinstituted prayer in schools, the crime rate would start to fall.

_____ 9. Athletes today make enormous salaries because they're overpaid.

_____ 10. If you don't make a donation to the United Way, you're a cheapskate.

Name: _____

Section_____ Date _____

SCORE: (Number correct) × 10 = _____%

ACTIVE READING AND STUDY: Test A

After reading the passage, write the letter of the best answer to each question.

A. [1]The tendency to overestimate the rarity of events is referred to as the overestimation effect. [2]Suppose a "psychic" comes to your class of 23 students. [3]Using his psychic abilities, the visitor "senses" that two people in the class were born on the same day. [4]A quick survey finds that, indeed, two people share the same month and date of birth. [5]This is pretty impressive evidence of psychic ability, right? [6]After all, what are the odds that two people in a class of 23 would have the same birthday? [7]When we perform this "psychic" demonstration in class, our students usually estimate that it is very unlikely that two people in a class of 23 will share a birthday. [8]In reality, the odds are 1 in 2, or 50–50. [9]Our students' overestimation of the rarity of the event is an example of the overestimation effect.

_____ 1. The key to the important ideas in this passage is
    A. a definition and an example.
    B. an enumeration.
    C. a definition and an enumeration.

_____ 2. Study notes on this selection should consist of
    A. the definition of the overestimation effect.
    B. the definition and an example of the overestimation effect.
    C. examples of the overestimation effect.

B. [1]In recent American political history, the media have played a central role in at least three major events. [2]First, the media were critically important factors in the civil rights movement of the 1950s and 1960s. [3]Television pictures showing peaceful civil rights marchers attacked by club-swinging police helped to generate sympathy among Northern whites for the civil rights struggle and greatly increased the pressure on Congress to bring an end to segregation. [4]Second, the media were instrumental in compelling the Johnson and Nixon administrations to negotiate an end to the Vietnam War. [5]Beginning in 1967, the national media portrayed the war as misguided and unwinnable and, as a result, helped to turn popular sentiment against continued American involvement. [6]Third, the media were central actors in the Watergate affair, which ultimately forced President Richard Nixon, landslide victor in the 1972 presidential election, to resign from office in disgrace. [7]It was the relentless series of investigations launched by the *Washington Post*, the *New York Times*, and the major television networks that led to the disclosures of the various abuses of which Nixon was guilty and ultimately forced Nixon to choose between resignation and almost certain impeachment.

_____ 3. The key to the important ideas in this passage is
    A. an enumeration.
    B. a definition.
    C. an enumeration and a definition.

_____ 4. Study notes on this selection should include
    A. the first and last sentence of the passage.
    B. major and minor details about the civil rights movement.
    C. a list of major events in which the media played a central role.

C. [1]Drawing on a large body of research, psychologists have identified three quite different types of stable or enduring marriages. [2]Validating couples have disagreements, but the disagreements rarely escalate. [3]The partners express mutual respect even when they disagree and listen well to one another. [4]Volatile couples squabble a lot, disagree, and don't listen to each other when they argue. [5]But they still have more positive than negative encounters and show high levels of laughter and affection. [6]Avoidant couples, or "conflict minimizers," don't try to persuade each other—they simply agree to disagree, without apparent rancor, a pattern that is sometimes described as "devitalized."

____ 5. The key to the important ideas in this passage is
    A. enumerations.
    B. an enumeration and definitions.
    C. definitions.

____ 6. Study notes on this selection should include
    A. real-life examples of validating, volatile, and avoidant couples.
    B. a list and definitions of the three types of stable or enduring marriages.
    C. the first and last sentence of the passage.

D. [1]Throughout almost all American history, New York has been the Great U.S. City. [2]It symbolizes the United States to the world and, in many ways, reveals the rest of the world to the United States. [3]Here are just a few of the features that make it so outstanding. [4]First, New York is huge, an enormous concentration of population. [5]Over 8 million people live within the city limits, and almost three times that many reside in the urban region that sprawls outward around the city. [6]Second, it has the nation's greatest concentration of business and finance: About one-tenth of the largest U.S. corporations have headquarters in Manhattan, and a huge percentage of all stocks and bonds are traded there; in addition, it is a major location for most international businesses located in North America. [7]Third, it is the largest U.S. port and has dominated American commerce since the early 1800s. [8]Fourth, it is a mosaic of virtually every race and ethnic group in the world—over 50 different foreign-language newspapers are published in the city. [9]Fifth, other New York districts are world-famous: Wall Street (finance), Madison Avenue (advertising), the garment district (center of the nation's clothing industry), Central Park, Fifth Avenue, Greenwich Village, and Broadway. [10]Sixth, New York is also a key center of the arts, music, and publishing.

____ 7. The key to the important ideas in this passage is
    A. an enumeration.
    B. definitions.
    C. an enumeration and definitions.

____ 8. Study notes on this selection should include
    A. a list of features that make New York outstanding.
    B. major and minor details about New York as a hub for business and finance.
    C. examples of New York districts.

E. *Facts and Fallacies about Depression*

[1]Although it is one of the fastest-growing problems in U.S. culture, depression remains one of the most misunderstood mental disorders. [2]Myths and misperceptions about the disease abound. [3]What follows are some facts about depression.

[4]*True depression is not a natural reaction to crisis and loss.* [5]It is a pervasive and systemic biological problem. [6]Symptoms may come and go, and their severity will fluctuate, but they do not simply go away. [7]Crisis and loss can lead an already depressed person over the edge to suicide or other problems, but crisis and loss do not inevitably result in depression.

[8]*People will not snap out of depression by "using a little willpower."* [9]Telling a depressed person to snap out of it is like telling a diabetic to produce more insulin. [10]Medical intervention in the form of antidepressant drugs and therapy is often necessary for recovery.

[11]*Frequent crying is not a hallmark of depression.* [12]Some people who are depressed bear their burdens in silence or may even be the life of the party. [13]Some depressed individuals don't cry at all. [14]Rather, biochemists theorize that crying may actually ward off depression by releasing chemicals that the body produces as a positive response to stress.

[15]*Depression is not all in the mind.* [16]Depression isn't a disease of weak-willed, powerless people. [17]In fact, research suggests that depressive illnesses originate with an inherited chemical imbalance in the brain. [18]In addition, some physiological conditions, such as thyroid disorders, multiple sclerosis, chronic fatigue syndrome, and certain cancers have depressive side effects. [19]Certain medications also are known to prompt depressive symptoms.

[20]*In-depth psychotherapy is not the only cure for long-term clinical depression.* [21]No single psychotherapy method works for all cases of depression.

_____ 9. The keys to the important ideas in this passage are
   A. enumerations.
   B. a title and subtitles.
   C. an enumeration and a heading and subheads.

_____ 10. Study notes on this selection should consist of
   A. the first and last sentence.
   B. signs that someone is truly depressed.
   C. facts which contradict myths about depression.

ACTIVE READING AND STUDY: Test B

After reading the passage, write the letter of the best answer to each question.

A. ¹The Abkhasians, an agricultural people who live in a mountainous region of Georgia, a republic of the former Soviet Union, may be the longest-lived people on Earth. ²Many claim to live past 100—some beyond 120 and even 130. ³Although it is difficult to document the accuracy of their claims, government records indicate that an extraordinary number of Abkhasians do live to a very old age. ⁴Three main factors appear to account for their long lives. ⁵The first is their diet, which consists of little meat, much fresh fruit, vegetables, garlic, goat cheese, cornmeal, buttermilk, and wine. ⁶The second is their lifelong physical activity. ⁷They do slow down after age 80, but even after the age of 100 they still work about four hours a day. ⁸The third factor— a highly developed sense of community—goes to the very heart of Abkhasian culture. ⁹From childhood, each individual is integrated into the primary group, and remains so throughout life. ¹⁰There is no such thing as a nursing home, nor do the elderly live alone. ¹¹Because they continue to work and contribute to the group's welfare, the elderly aren't a burden to anyone. ¹²They don't vegetate, nor do they feel the need to "fill time" with bingo and shuffleboard. ¹³In short, the elderly feel no sudden rupture between what they "were" and what they "are."

____ 1. The key to the important ideas in this passage is
   A. an enumeration.
   B. a definition.
   C. an enumeration and a definition.

____ 2. Study notes on this selection should include
   A. the first and last sentence of the passage.
   B. major and minor details about the Abkhasians' attitude toward the elderly.
   C. a list of reasons why the Abkhasians live so long.

B. *Kohlberg and the Stages of Moral Development*

¹Lawrence Kohlberg elaborated on Piaget's theories of cognitive reasoning by conducting a series of studies in which children, adolescents, and adults were presented with moral dilemmas that took the form of stories. ²Based on his findings, Kohlberg classified moral reasoning into three sequential levels:

1. *Preconventional level* (ages seven to ten). ³Children's perceptions are based on punishment and obedience. ⁴Evil behavior is that which is likely to be punished; good conduct is based on obedience and avoidance of unwanted consequences.

2. *Conventional level* (age ten through adulthood). ⁵People are most concerned with how they are perceived by their peers and with how one conforms to rules.

3. *Postconventional level* (few adults reach this stage). ⁶People view morality in terms of individual rights; "moral conduct" is judged by principles based on human rights that transcend government and laws.

____ 3. The keys to the important ideas in this passage are
   A. enumerations.
   B. a title and subtitles.
   C. an enumeration and a heading and subheads.

___ 4. Study notes on this selection should consist of
    A. the first and last sentence.
    B. definitions and examples of each of the levels of moral reasoning.
    C. a list of the levels of moral reasoning and a brief description of each.

C. [1]When you purchase tickets for an airplane flight or a movie, you are subjected to a common incentive scheme called "peak-load pricing." [2]The idea of peak-load pricing is to create incentives for customers to demand goods and services when supply is ample and not when supply is short. [3]Taking this approach, restaurants often provide low prices before 6 P.M., and tropical resorts offer discounts in the summer to spread their patronage out—a cheaper solution than expanding to accommodate more customers during the peak season. [4]Similarly, happy hour drink prices in bars would more aptly be called quiet hour prices because they create incentives for patrons to visit during what otherwise would be slow periods.

___ 5. The key to the important ideas in this passage is
    A. a definition.
    B. a definition and examples.
    C. a definition and an enumeration.

___ 6. Study notes on this selection should include
    A. a definition of peak-load pricing.
    B. an example of peak-load pricing.
    C. the definition and an example of peak-load pricing.

D. [1]Just as many students use contact lenses or glasses to help them compensate for poor eyesight, students with disabilities may rely on a variety of technology-based innovations to help them learn better. [2]The term *assistive technology* refers to the array of devices and services that help people with disabilities perform better in their daily lives. [3]Devices such as motorized chairs, remote control units to turn on appliances, voice recognition systems, ramps to enter and exit buildings, and computers can all assist people with severe disabilities. [4]Computers are especially important in allowing many students with a range of disabilities to participate in normal classroom activities that would otherwise be impossible.

___ 7. The key to the important ideas in this passage is
    A. a definition.
    B. a definition and examples.
    C. an enumeration.

___ 8. Study notes in this selection should consist of
    A. examples of assistive technology.
    B. the definition and an example of assistive technology.
    C. a list of various types of disabilities.

E. [1]The beneficial effects of stress may prove more difficult to pinpoint than the harmful effects because they may be more subtle. [2]Although research data are sparse, there appear to be at least three ways in which stress can have positive effects. [3]First, stressful events help satisfy the need for stimulation and challenge. [4]Studies suggest that most people need an intermediate level of stimulation and challenge in their lives. [5]Although we think of stress in terms of stimulus overload, underload can be stressful as well. [6]Thus, most people would experience a suffocating level of boredom if they lived a stress-free existence. [7]Second, stress can promote personal growth or self-improvement. [8]For example, studies of people grappling with major health problems show that the majority report having derived benefits from their adversity. [9]Stressful events sometimes force people to develop new skills, reevaluate priorities, learn new insights, and acquire new strengths. [10]In other words, the adaptation process initiated by stress may lead to personal changes that are changes for the better. [11]Third, today's stress can inoculate individuals so that they are less affected by tomorrow's stress. [12]Some studies suggest that exposure to stress can increase stress tolerance—as long as the stress isn't overwhelming.

____ 9. The key to the important ideas in this passage is
   A. a definition.
   B. a definition and enumerations.
   C. an enumeration.

____ 10. Study notes on this selection should include
   A. the first and last sentence.
   B. major and minor details about how stress can promote personal growth.
   C. a list of ways that stress can prove beneficial.

ACTIVE READING AND STUDY: Test C

After reading the passage, write the letter of the best answer to each question.

A. [1]Derived from the word *ethnos* (a Greek word meaning "people" or "nation"), *ethnicity* and *ethnic* refer to people who identify with one another on the basis of common ancestry and cultural heritage. [2]Their sense of belonging may center on their nation of origin, distinctive foods, dress, language, music, religion, or family names and relationships. [3]People often confuse the terms *race* and *ethnic group*. [4]For example, many people, including many Jews, consider the Jews a race. [5]Jews, however, are more properly considered an ethnic group, for it is their cultural characteristics, especially their religion, that bind them together. [6]Wherever Jews have lived in the world, they have intermarried. [7]Consequently, Jews in China may look mongoloid, while some Swedish Jews are blue-eyed blonds.

____ 1. The keys to the important ideas in this passage are
    A. enumerations.
    B. definitions and an example.
    C. an enumeration and definitions.

____ 2. Study notes on this selection should include
    A. major and minor details about races and ethnic groups.
    B. examples of Jewish customs.
    C. the definition of *ethnicity* (or *ethnic*) and an example of an ethnic group.

B. [1]Psychologist Lenore Walker developed a theory known as the "cycle of violence" to explain how women can get caught in a downward spiral of abuse without knowing what is happening to them. [2]The cycle has three phases. [3]The first phase is tension building. [4]In this phase, minor battering occurs, and the woman may become more nurturant, more pleasing, and more intent on anticipating the spouse's needs in order to forestall more violence. [5]She assumes guilt for doing something to provoke him and tries hard to avoid doing it again. [6]The second phase is acute battery. [7]At this stage, pleasing her man doesn't help, and she can no longer control or predict the abuse. [8]Usually, the spouse is trying to "teach her a lesson," and when he feels he has inflicted enough pain, he'll stop. [9]When the acute attack is over, he may respond with shock and denial about his own behavior. [10]Both batterer and victim may soft-pedal the seriousness of the attacks. [11]The final phase is remorse/reconciliation. [12]During this "honeymoon" period, the batterer may be kind, loving, and apologetic, swearing he will never act violently again. [13]He may stop his violent behavior for several weeks or months, and the woman may come to question whether she overreacted. [14]When the tension that precipitated past abuses resurfaces, the man beats the woman again. [15]Unless some form of intervention breaks the downward cycle of abuse, it will repeat itself again and again and perhaps end only with the woman's—or, rarely, the man's—death.

____ 3. The keys to the important ideas in this passage are
    A. definitions and examples.
    B. definitions.
    C. enumerations.

____ 4. Study notes on this selection should consist of
    A. the definition of *domestic abuse*.
    B. reasons why women become abused.
    C. a list of the three phases of the "cycle of abuse" and a brief definition (description) of each.

C. [1]Since there is only so much 654,601 police officers can do to monitor the activities of nearly 300 million people, the police exercise considerable discretion about what situations warrant their attention and how to handle them. [2]How, then, do police carry out their duties? [3]Researchers have concluded that, because they must act swiftly, police quickly size up situations in terms of six factors. [4]First, the more serious they think the situation is, the more likely they are to make an arrest. [5]Second, police take account of the victim's wishes in deciding whether to make an arrest. [6]Third, the odds of arrest go up the more uncooperative a suspect is. [7]Fourth, police are more likely to take into custody someone they have arrested before, presumably because this suggests guilt. [8]Fifth, the presence of bystanders increases the chances of arrest. [9]According to researchers, the presence of observers prompts police to take stronger control of a situation, if only to move the encounter from the street (the suspect's turf) to the police department (where law enforcement officers have the edge). [10]Sixth, all else being equal, police are more likely to arrest people of color than white, perceiving people of African or Latino descent as either more dangerous or more likely to be guilty.

___ 5. The keys to the important ideas in this passage are
   A. enumerations.
   B. definitions.
   C. an enumeration and definitions.

___ 6. Study notes on this selection should include
   A. a list of factors affecting how police carry out their duties.
   B. examples of the ways that police fight serious crime.
   C. how police define the word *duty*.

D. [1]Sibling relationships vary enormously. [2]On the basis of direct studies of young children as well as retrospective reports by young adults about their sibling relationships when they were of school age, researchers have identified several patterns, or styles, of sibling relationships:

- [3]A caregiver relationship, in which one sibling serves as a kind of quasi-parent for the other (this pattern seems to be more common between an older sister and a younger brother than for any other combination).
- [4]A buddy relationship, in which both members of the pair try to be like each other and take pleasure in being together.
- [5]A critical, or conflicted relationship, which includes teasing, quarreling, and attempts by one sibling to dominate the other.
- [6]A rival relationship, which contains many of the same elements as a critical relationship but is also low in any form of friendliness or support.
- [7]A casual relationship, in which the siblings have relatively little to do with one another.

___ 7. The key to the important ideas in this passage is
   A. a definition and examples.
   B. an enumeration.
   C. an enumeration and definitions.

___ 8. Study notes on this selection should consist of
   A. the definition of *sibling*.
   B. a list of patterns or styles of sibling relationships.
   C. examples of conflicted and casual sibling relationships.

E. [1]War exacts many costs in addition to killing people and destroying property. [2]One is its effect on morality. [3]Exposure to brutality and killing often causes dehumanization, the process of reducing people to objects that do not deserve to be treated as humans.

[4]As we review findings on dehumanization and see how it breeds callousness and cruelty, perhaps we can better understand why "good people" can dehumanize others. [5]Consider four characteristics of dehumanization:

1. Increased emotional distance from others. [6]People stop identifying with others, no longer seeing them as having qualities similar to themselves. [7]They often perceive them as "the enemy," or as objects of some sort, and sometimes as subhuman, not as people at all.

2. An emphasis on following procedures. [8]Regulations are not questioned, for they are seen as a means to an end. [9]People are likely to say, "I don't like doing this, but I have to follow rules," or "We all have to die some day. [10]What difference does it make if these people die now?"

3. Inability to resist pressures. [11]One's own ideas of morality take a back seat to fears of losing one's job, losing the respect of one's peers, or having one's integrity and loyalty questioned.

4. A diminished sense of personal responsibility. [12]People come to see themselves as only small cogs in a large machine. [13]They are not responsible for what they do, for they are simply following orders. [14]The higher-ups who give the orders are thought to have more complete or even secret information that justifies what is being done. [15]They think, "The higher-ups are in a position to judge what is right and wrong, but in my humble place, who am I to question these acts?"

_____ 9. The key to the important ideas in this passage is
    A. a definition and examples.
    B. a definition and an enumeration.
    C. an enumeration.

_____ 10. Study notes on this selection should consist of
    A. the definition of *dehumanization*.
    B. the definition and an example of dehumanization.
    C. the definition of *dehumanization* and a list of characteristics of dehumanization.

ACTIVE READING AND STUDY: Test D

After reading the passage, write the letter of the best answer to each question.

A. [1]If there is no single point at which people automatically cross a magic line and become "old," what, then, makes someone "old"? [2]We can point to several factors that spur people to apply the label of "old" to themselves. [3]The first factor is biology. [4]One person may experience "signs" of aging earlier than others: wrinkles, balding, aches, difficulty in doing something that he or she used to take for granted. [5]Consequently, one person will feel "old" at an earlier or a later age than others. [6]A second factor is personal history or biography. [7]A woman who gave birth at 16 may have a daughter who in turn has a child at 18, making the woman a biological grandparent at age 34. [8]It is most unlikely that she will begin to play any stereotypical role—spending the day in a rocking chair, for example—but knowing that she is a grandmother has an impact on her self-concept. [9]At a minimum, she must deny that she is old. [10]An accident that limits someone's mobility may also make that person feel older sooner than others. [11]Then there is gender age, the relative value that a culture places on men's and women's ages. [12]For example, graying hair on men, even some wrinkles, may be seen as signs of "maturity"; on women, those same features can be interpreted as being "old."

[13]The fourth factor in deciding when people label themselves as "old" is timetables, the signals societies use to inform their members that old age has begun. [14]Since there is no automatic age at which people become "old," these timetables vary around the world. [15]One group may choose a particular birthday, such as the 60th or 65th, to signal the onset of old age. [16]Other groups do not even have birthdays, making such numbers meaningless. [17]In the West, retirement is sometimes a cultural signal of the beginning of old age—which is one reason that some people resist retirement.

____ 1. The key to the important ideas in this passage is
    A. a definition.
    B. a definition and examples and an enumeration.
    C. an enumeration.

____ 2. Study notes on this selection should consist of
    A. a list of factors which cause people to call themselves "old."
    B. examples of various elderly people.
    C. the first and last sentence.

B. *Behavior During the Interview*

[1]Interviewing can be stressful. [2]Use these guidelines to help you put your best foot forward.

1. Use active listening. [3]When we are anxious, we sometimes have trouble listening well. [4]Work on attending, understanding, and remembering what is asked. [5]Remember that the interviewer will be aware of your nonverbal behavior, so be sure to make and keep eye contact as you listen.

2. Think before answering. [6]If you have prepared for the interview, you want to make sure that as you answer the questions posed, you also tell your story. [7]So take a moment to consider how your answer will portray your skills and experiences. [8]"Tell me about yourself" is not an invitation to give the interviewer your life history. [9]Rather, you can focus your answer on presenting your experiences and qualifications that are related to the job.

3. Be enthusiastic. [10]If you come across as bored or uninterested, the interviewer is likely to conclude that you would be an unmotivated employee.

4. Ask questions. ¹¹As the interviewer is winding down, be sure to ask the questions you prepared that have not already been answered. ¹²You may also want to ask how well the interviewer believes your qualifications match the position and tell the interviewer what your strengths are.

5. Avoid discussing salary and benefits. ¹³The time to discuss salary is when you are offered the job. ¹⁴If the interviewer tries to pin you down, simply say something like, "I'm really more interested in talking about how my experiences map onto your needs and would like to defer talking about salary until we know we have a match."

___ 3. The keys to the important ideas in this passage are
  A. enumerations.
  B. a title and subtitles.
  C. an enumeration and a heading and subheads.

___ 4. Study notes on this selection should consist of
  A. the first and last sentence.
  B. examples of "trick" interview questions.
  C. things to do and not do during an interview.

C. ¹Suppose that, after graduating from college, you have two options: to go to school for an additional year to get an advanced degree, or to take a job immediately. ²You would like to take the extra year in school but are concerned about the cost. ³This cost, like any cost, can be broken into two parts: the explicit cost of the year's schooling and the implicit cost. ⁴An explicit cost is a cost that requires an outlay of money. ⁵For example, the explicit cost of the additional year of schooling includes tuition. ⁶An implicit cost, on the other hand, does not involve any outlay of money; instead, it is measured by the value, in dollar terms, of all the benefits that are foregone. ⁷For example, the implicit cost of the year spent in school includes the income you would have earned if you had taken that job instead.

___ 5. The keys to the important ideas in this passage are
  A. enumerations.
  B. definitions and examples.
  C. definitions and an enumeration.

___ 6. Study notes on this selection should include
  A. definitions.
  B. the first and last sentence.
  C. definitions and an example.

D. ¹Researchers have concluded that about two-thirds of babies can be classified into one of three broad temperamental patterns: easy, difficult, and slow-to-warm-up. ²About a third of the infants were characterized as average babies because they did not fit neatly into one of these three categories. ³Easy babies readily adapt to new experiences, generally display positive moods and emotions, and have regular sleeping and eating patterns. ⁴Difficult babies tend to be intensely emotional, are irritable and fussy, and cry a lot. ⁵They also tend to have irregular sleeping and eating patterns. ⁶Slow-to-warm-up babies have a low activity level, withdraw from new situations and people, and adapt to new experiences very gradually.

___ 7. The keys to the important ideas in this passage are
  A. an example and definitions.
  B. enumerations.
  C. definitions.

___ 8. Study notes on this selection should consist of
  A. the definition of *temperament*.
  B. the first and last sentence.
  C. a list of three types of babies and a definition (description) of each type.

E. [1]Ethnocentrism is the belief that our own group or culture—whatever it may be—is superior to all other groups or cultures. [2]Because of ethnocentrism, we identify with our group or culture and see its values, beliefs, and customs as "right" or "natural"—in comparison to the values, beliefs, and customs of other groups or cultures, which we tend to think of as "wrong" or "unnatural." [3]If you were born and raised in the United States, you might find it strange that most people in India regard the cow as a sacred animal and forego using it as a source of food. [4]On the other hand, if you were born and raised in India, you might well be shocked at the use of cows in the United States for food, clothing, and other consumer goods. [5]If you are Christian, you most likely think of Sunday as the "normal" day of worship. [6]But if you are Jewish, you probably regard Saturday as the "correct" Sabbath. [7]And if you are Muslim, you doubtless see both Saturday and Sunday as unusual times for worship. For you, Friday is the "right" day.

___ 9. The key to the important ideas in this passage is
  A. a definition and examples.
  B. an enumeration.
  C. a definition and an enumeration.

___ 10. Study notes on this selection should consist of
  A. the definition of *ethnocentrism*.
  B. the definition and an example of ethnocentrism.
  C. examples of ethnocentrism.

COMBINED SKILLS: Test A

After reading the passage, write the letter of the best answer to each question.

[1]Today many of us take for granted easy access to consumer goods via local shopping malls and the Internet. [2]But in the late 1800s, the only access people in isolated rural communities had to consumer goods was through the mail-order catalogs of retailers Montgomery Ward and Sears, Roebuck. [3]"The Montgomery Ward catalog," declared a farm woman in Nebraska, "was a real link between us and civilization." [4]Ward's catalog, only eight pages long when the business was launched, mushroomed to 540 pages, offering 24,000 items, by the 1880s; at the turn of the century, it was 1,200 pages, with 17,000 illustrations. [5]The catalog offered farm families virtually every kind of product made in the United States: from gasoline stoves, bicycles, and batteries to dresses, underwear, and carriages, to toys, carpets, artworks, and pianos. [6]Farm families, after placing their orders, sent their payments in advance or paid at a local freight desk once their orders were received; by 1900, Ward was receiving between 15,000 and 35,000 letters a day, some from towns as remote as Bywy, Mississippi. [7]Thanks to the catalogs, farmers were able to acquire goods that had been rare or unknown in rural America: ready-made clothing, Aunt Jemima's pancake flour, hams, foodstuffs made by Heinz and Pillsbury, furniture, musical instruments, tools, and barbed wire so that they no longer had to build fences from hand-wrought rails. [8]And by giving farm families a glimpse of an urban style of living, the catalogs altered the tastes and reshaped the desires of many rural Americans.

_____ 1. According to the author, farm families paid for their catalog orders
    A. by making installment payments.
    B. in advance or when the order was received at a local freight office.
    C. in advance or when the order was delivered to their door.
    D. by taking out a bank loan.

_____ 2. According to the selection, which of the following was *not* rare or unknown in rural America before mail-order catalogs?
    A. Aunt Jemima's pancake flour.
    B. musical instruments.
    C. barbed wire.
    D. hand-wrought rails.

_____ 3. The relationship of sentence 2 to sentence 1 is one of
    A. cause and effect.
    B. contrast.
    C. time order.
    D. addition.

_____ 4. Sentence 4 expresses a relationship of
    A. contrast.
    B. comparison.
    C. illustration.
    D. time.

_____ 5. We can infer from this selection that people in isolated rural communities
      A. often could not read or write.
      B. at times felt cut off from civilization.
      C. were uncivilized.
      D. had little money to spend on consumer goods.

_____ 6. This selection suggests that in the 1800s, the United States
      A. was fast becoming a manufacturing powerhouse.
      B. was a nation made up entirely of small farms.
      C. had to import many manufactured goods from overseas.
      D. had no large cities.

_____ 7. In sentence 3, the tone of the farm woman in Nebraska is
      A. amused.
      B. detached.
      C. appreciative.
      D. nostalgic.

_____ 8. This passage is mainly made up of
      A. facts.
      B. opinions.

_____ 9. The author's primary purpose is to
      A. question.
      B. praise.
      C. inform.
      D. entertain.

_____ 10. Which is the most appropriate title for this selection?
      A. Rural America in the 1800s
      B. The Rise of Retail Giants Montgomery Ward and Sears
      C. How to Sell Goods to Rural Communities
      D. How Mail-Order Catalogs Benefited Rural America

TEN STEPS TO
ADVANCED READING

COMBINED SKILLS: Test B

After reading the passage, write the letter of the best answer to each question.

[1]Under what conditions is helping behavior most likely to occur? [2]The most important situational variable is the presence of other people. [3]In a phenomenon called the bystander effect, the likelihood that a person will help someone else in trouble decreases as the number of bystanders present increases. [4]In one experiment, people filling out a questionnaire heard a taped "emergency" in the next room, complete with a crash and screams. [5]Of those who were alone, 70% offered help to the unseen female victim, but of those who waited with a companion—a stranger who did nothing to help—only 7% offered help. [6]Another key aspect of the situation is its ambiguity. [7]Any factors that make it harder for others to recognize a genuine emergency reduce the probability of helping behavior. [8]The personal characteristics of bystanders also affect helping behavior. [9]Not all bystanders are equally likely to help a stranger. [10]Increasing the amount of personal responsibility that one person feels for another boosts the likelihood that help will be extended. [11]The amount of empathy affects our behavior, too; the more we identify with someone, the more willing we are to help that person. [12]Mood also makes a difference: A person in a good mood is more likely to help another in need than is someone who is in a neutral or bad mood. [13]In addition, helping behavior is increased when people don't fear embarrassment by offering assistance that isn't really needed. [14]Finally, when others are watching, people who score high on the need for approval are more likely to help than are low scorers.

____ 1. In sentence 6, the word *ambiguity* means
   A. reasonableness.
   B. logic.
   C. uncertainty.
   D. danger.

____ 2. In sentence 11, the word *empathy* means
   A. distrust.
   B. understanding.
   C. anger.
   D. confusion.

____ 3. According to the passage, the fact that only 7% of the people who waited with a companion offered to help an unseen victim
   A. shows that people are basically selfish.
   B. disproves the bystander effect.
   C. happened because 93% of the people realized that the "emergency" wasn't real.
   D. illustrates the bystander effect.

____ 4. The relationship of sentence 6 to sentence 5 is one of
   A. illustration.
   B. time.
   C. addition.
   D. comparison.

_____ 5. The main pattern of organization of the passage is
   A. time order.
   B. list of items.
   C. cause and effect.
   D. contrast.

_____ 6. The passage suggests that some people help others because
   A. they want others to see them in a positive light.
   B. they recognize that a person in trouble really does need help.
   C. they like, or value, the person who needs help.
   D. all of the above.

_____ 7. Based on the passage, we can infer that someone who is depressed would be
   A. less likely to help someone in trouble.
   B. more likely to help someone in trouble.
   C. just as likely to help someone in trouble as if he or she were not depressed.
   D. too embarrassed to help someone in trouble.

_____ 8. The author's primary purpose is to
   A. entertain.
   B. inform.
   C. persuade.
   D. question.

_____ 9. Sentences 4 and 5 state
   A. facts.
   B. opinions.

_____ 10. Which statement best expresses the central point of the selection?
   A. People will help others only under very special circumstances.
   B. People are much less likely to help others if other people are present.
   C. The personal characteristics of bystanders affect helping behavior.
   D. There are a number of factors which affect whether or not helping behavior will occur.

COMBINED SKILLS: Test C

After reading the passage, write the letter of the best answer to each question.

[1]In the early days of European settlement, the colonies that would become the United States used commodity money, consisting in part of gold and silver coins. [2]But such coins were scarce on this side of the Atlantic, so the colonists relied on a variety of other forms of commodity money. [3]For example, settlers in Virginia used tobacco as money, and settlers in the Northeast used "wampum," a type of clamshell.

[4]Later in American history, commodity-backed paper money came into widespread use. [5]But this wasn't paper money as we now know it, issued by the government and bearing the signature of the Secretary of the Treasury. [6]Before the Civil War, the U.S. government didn't issue paper money at all. [7]Dollar bills were issued by private banks, which promised holders that these bills could be redeemed for silver coins on demand. [8]These promises weren't always credible because sometimes banks failed. [9]People were reluctant to accept currency from banks suspected of being in financial trouble. [10]In other words, some dollars were less valuable than others.

[11]The U.S. government began issuing official paper money, called "greenbacks," during the Civil War. [12]At first greenbacks had no fixed value in terms of commodities. [13]After 1873 the U.S. government guaranteed the value of a dollar in terms of gold, effectively turning dollars into commodity-backed money.

[14]In 1933, when President Franklin D. Roosevelt broke the link between dollars and gold, his own federal budget director declared ominously, "This will be the end of Western civilization." [15]It wasn't. [16]The link between the dollar and gold was restored a few years later, then dropped again—seemingly for good—in August 1971. [17]Despite the warnings of doom, the U.S. dollar is still the world's most widely used currency.

____ 1. In sentence 8, the word *credible* means
   A. understandable.
   B. honest.
   C. necessary.
   D. believable.

____ 2. According to the passage, dollar bills issued by private banks
   A. were worth more than "greenbacks."
   B. competed with gold and silver coins.
   C. varied in value due to the strength or weakness of the bank which issued them.
   D. were usually worthless.

____ 3. According to the passage, today
   A. the U.S. dollar is commodity-backed money.
   B. some dollars are less valuable than others.
   C. there is no link between U.S. dollars and gold.
   D. people in other countries are reluctant to accept the U.S. dollar as currency.

____ 4. The relationship of sentence 3 to sentence 2 is one of
   A. illustration.
   B. addition.
   C. time.
   D. cause and effect.

_____ 5. The relationship of sentence 17 to sentences 14–16 is one of
    A. cause and effect.
    B. contrast.
    C. illustration.
    D. time.

_____ 6. We can infer that the early colonists used tobacco and "wampum" as money because
    A. these items were readily available.
    B. these items were very valuable.
    C. these items were common all over Europe as well as America.
    D. all of the above.

_____ 7. The author suggests that
    A. it was a mistake for President Franklin Roosevelt to break the link between dollars and gold.
    B. in the future, the link between dollars and gold will be re-established.
    C. it is not necessary for U.S. dollars to be backed by gold.
    D. the U.S. economy has declined steadily since August 1971.

_____ 8. The tone of this passage is
    A. critical.
    B. instructive.
    C. humorous.
    D. scornful.

_____ 9. Which sentence best expresses the central point of the passage?
    A. U.S. currency should be backed by gold.
    B. U.S. currency has gone through a number of changes since colonial times.
    C. Bank-issued currency was a failure in the United States.
    D. Modern American money got its start when the U.S. government began issuing greenbacks.

_____ 10. What is the most appropriate title for this selection?
    A. The Origins of Paper Money
    B. The Origins of Commodity Money
    C. Our Changing Currency
    D. Why the U.S. Dollar Is the World's Most Widely Used Currency

COMBINED SKILLS: Test D

After reading the passage, write the letter of the best answer to each question.

[1]"Two heads are better than one" reflects the common assumption that members of a group will pool their abilities and arrive at a better decision than will individuals working alone. [2]In fact, groups are more effective than individuals only under certain circumstances. [3]For one thing, their success depends on the task they face. [4]If the requirements of the task match the skills of the group members, the group is likely to be more effective than any single individual.

[5]Even if task and personnel are perfectly matched, however, the ways in which group members interact may reduce the group's efficiency. [6]For example, high-status individuals tend to exert more influence in groups, so if they do not possess the best problem-solving skills, group decisions may suffer. [7]Another factor affecting group interaction and effectiveness is group size. [8]The larger the group, the more likely it is to include someone who has the skills needed to solve a difficult problem. [9]On the other hand, it is much harder to coordinate the activities of a large group. [10]In addition, large groups may be more likely to encourage social loafing, the tendency of group members to exert less individual effort on the assumption that others in the group will do the work. [11]Finally, the quality of group decision-making also depends on the cohesiveness of a group. [12]When the people in a group like one another and feel committed to the goals of the group, cohesiveness is high. [13]Under these conditions, members may work hard for the group, spurred by high morale. [14]But cohesiveness can undermine the quality of group decision-making. [15]If the group succumbs to groupthink, strong pressure to conform prevents its members from criticizing the emerging group consensus. [16]In such a group, amiability and morale supersede judgment. [17]Members with doubts may hesitate to express them. [18]The result may be disastrous decisions—such as the Bay of Pigs invasion, the Watergate burglary and cover-up, or the ill-fated *Columbia* and *Challenger* space flights.

____ 1. In sentence 11, the word *cohesiveness* means
   A. abilities.
   B. tendency to stick together.
   C. intelligence.
   D. trustworthiness.

____ 2. In sentence 15, the word *succumbs* means
   A. gives in.
   B. agrees.
   C. advances.
   D. refers.

____ 3. According to the selection,
   A. a large group is always more effective than a small group.
   B. a large group is generally less effective than a small group.
   C. there are both advantages and disadvantages to large groups.
   D. no group should be larger than eight people.

____ 4. According to the selection, large groups may be more likely to encourage
   A. social loafing.
   B. groupthink.
   C. high morale.
   D. all of the above.

_____ 5. The relationship of sentence 7 to sentence 6 is one of
   A. illustration.
   B. addition.
   C. time.
   D. cause and effect.

_____ 6. The relationship of sentence 14 to sentence 13 is one of
   A. cause and effect.
   B. time.
   C. illustration.
   D. contrast.

_____ 7. TRUE OR FALSE? The passage suggests that tragic errors such as the Bay of Pigs invasion and the *Columbia* and *Challenger* disasters could have been prevented if members of each decision-making group had expressed their doubts of the mission's success.

_____ 8. We can infer from this passage that group leaders should
   A. encourage group members to voice any disagreements they may have about a proposed course of action.
   B. strive above all to encourage group cohesiveness.
   C. value the opinions of high-status group members over the opinions of group members who do not possess high status.
   D. demand that group members conform to the wishes of the majority.

_____ 9. The passage suggests that
   A. groups with high morale usually make good decisions.
   B. high-status individuals tend to possess the best problem-solving skills.
   C. groups composed of people from similar backgrounds are preferable to groups composed of people from different backgrounds.
   D. groups aren't necessarily better at solving problems than individuals.

_____ 10. Which is the most appropriate title for this selection?
   A. How to Function Effectively in a Group
   B. Disastrous Group Decisions
   C. One Head Is Better Than Two
   D. Benefits and Drawbacks of Group Problem-Solving

ANSWERS TO THE TESTS IN THE TEST BANK

MAIN IDEAS: Test A

1. 1
2. 5
3. 2

4. 3
5. 8

MAIN IDEAS: Test B

1. 2
2. 8
3. 14

4. 2
5. 1

MAIN IDEAS: Test C

1. 3
2. 1
3. 11

4. 1
5. 2 or 15

MAIN IDEAS: Test D

1. 2
2. 7
3. 3

4. 1
5. 1

SUPPORTING DETAILS: Test A

A.
1. A
2. B
3. C
4. B
5. One *or* Another *or* third *or* also *or* final

B. (6–10.) *(Wording of answers may vary.)*
Main idea: In America there are four major ideological types.
- Conservatives: oppose an activist role for government in providing economic benefits but look to government to uphold traditional social values.
- Liberals: favor activist government as an instrument of economic redistribution but reject the notion that government should favor a particular set of social values.
- Populists: share conservatives' concern for traditional values but, like liberals, favor an active role for government in providing economic security.
- Libertarians: those who are opposed to governmental intervention in both the economic and social spheres.

SUPPORTING DETAILS: Test B

A.
1. A
2. C
3. C
4. B
5. One *or* Another *or* Finally

B. (6–10.) *(Wording of answers may vary.)*
Main idea: The development of a global economy has four major consequences.
- A global division of labor—different regions of the world specialize in one or another sector of economic activity.
- An increasing number of global products pass through more than one nation.
- National governments no longer control the economic activity that takes place within their borders.
- A small number of businesses control a vast share of the world's economic activity.

SUPPORTING DETAILS: Test C

A.
1. A
2. B
3. C
4. C
5. C

B. (6–10.) *(Wording of answers may vary.)*
Main idea: According to Anti-Slavery International, there are four types of slavery in the world today.
- Chattel slavery—one person owns another
- Child slavery—children do what they must to survive
- Debt bondage—workers are paid too little
- Servile forms of marriage—women married against their will and forced to work for their husband's family

SUPPORTING DETAILS: Test D

A.
1. A
2. C
3. C
4. B
5. first *or* second *or* final

B.
6. C
7. B
8. B
9. C
10. B

127

IMPLIED MAIN IDEAS: Test A

1. D   3. B
2. B   4. C

IMPLIED MAIN IDEAS: Test B

1. C   3. C
2. A   4. B

IMPLIED MAIN IDEAS: Test C

1. B   3. A
2. B   4. C

IMPLIED MAIN IDEAS: Test D

1. D   3. B
2. D   4. B

RELATIONSHIPS I: Test A

A.
1. A
2. D
3. B
4. C
5. E

B.
6. B, first
7. D, When
8. C, second
9. A, During
10. B

RELATIONSHIPS I: Test B

A.
1. B
2. D
3. E
4. C
5. A

B.
6. B, following
7. A, during
8. D, When
9. C, immediately
10. B

RELATIONSHIPS I: Test C

A.
1. A
2. C
3. D
4. E
5. B

B.
6. B, For one thing
7. D, Secondly
8. A, Another
9. C, Moreover
10. A

RELATIONSHIPS I: Test D

A.
1. A

2–4. • From tangible products to ideas
    • From mechanical skills to literacy skills
    • Work can now be done almost anywhere

B.
5. E, until
6. D, first
7. B, during
8. A, After
9. C, Eventually
10. B

RELATIONSHIPS II: Test A

A.
1. D
2. A
3. C
4. E
5. B

B.
6. D
7. A
8. B
9. D
10. A

RELATIONSHIPS II: Test B

A.
1. A
2. C
3. E
4. D
5. B

B.
6. C
7. D
8. A
9. B
10. A

RELATIONSHIPS II: Test C

A.
1. B
2. causes *or* cause *or* thus *or* result

B.
3. A
4. for example *or* for instance

C.
5. D
6. But *or* different *or* However *or* whereas

D.
7. D
8. By contrast *or* On the other hand

RELATIONSHIPS II: Test D

A.
1. B
2. Thus *or* effect

B.
3. D
4. differences *or* in contrast

C.
5. A
6. such as

D.
1. B
2. As a result *or* Since *or* Therefore

INFERENCES: Test A

1–2.	B, D	7–8.	B, C
3–4.	B, D	9–10.	B, C
5–6.	A, B		

INFERENCES: Test B

1–2.	A, D	7–8.	B, C
3–4.	A, D	9–10.	A, B
5–6.	A, B		

INFERENCES: Test C

1–5.	B	6–10.	A
	E		B
	F		E
	G		G
	J		H

INFERENCES: Test D

1–5.	A	6–10.	A
	C		B
	D		D
	G		H
	H		I

PURPOSE AND TONE: Test A

A.
1.	I	**B.**	7.	D
2.	E		8.	C
3.	P		9.	E
4.	E		10.	B
5.	P			
6.	I			

PURPOSE AND TONE: Test B

1.	B	6.	C
2.	A	7.	H
3.	F	8.	G
4.	E	9.	J
5.	D	10.	I

PURPOSE AND TONE: Test C

A.
1. B
2. C

B.
3. B
4. A

C. 5. C

PURPOSE AND TONE: Test D

A.
1. B
2. B

B.
3. C
4. C

C. 5. B

ARGUMENT: Test A

A.
1. C
2. B
3. D
4. A

B. 5. B

ARGUMENT: Test B

A.
1. B
2. C
3. B

B.
4. B
5. A

ARGUMENT: Test C

A.
1. D
2. B

B.
3–5. C, D, E
6–8. A, C, F

ARGUMENT: Test D

A. 1. D

B. 2. B

C. 3–5. A, C, F

CRITICAL READING: Test A

1. F		11.	F+O
2. O		12.	F
3. O		13.	O
4. F		14.	O
5. F		15.	F
6. O		16.	O
7. O		17.	F
8. F		18.	O
9. F		19.	F
10. O		20.	F

CRITICAL READING: Test B

A.	1. D	**B.**	7. D
	2. C		8. C
	3. B		9. A
	4. D		10. B
	5. C		
	6. B		

CRITICAL READING: Test C

A.	1. C	**B.**	6. C
	2. A		7. B
	3. B		8. A
	4. A		9. B
	5. C		10. A

CRITICAL READING: Test D

A.	1. F	**B.**	4. C	**C.**	8. D
	2. O		5. D		9. A
	3. F		6. A		10. F
			7. B		

ACTIVE READING: Test A

A.	1. A	**B.**	3. A	**C.**	5. B
	2. B		4. C		6. B
D.	7. A	**E.**	9. C		
	8. A		10. C		

ACTIVE READING: Test B

A.	1. A	**B.**	3. C	**C.**	5. B
	2. C		4. C		6. C
D.	7. B	**E.**	9. C		
	8. B		10. C		

ACTIVE READING: Test C

A.	1. B	**B.**	3. B	**C.**	5. A
	2. C		4. C		6. A
D.	7. C	**E.**	9. B		
	8. B		10. C		

ACTIVE READING: Test D

A.	1. C	**B.**	3. C	**C.**	5. B
	2. A		4. C		6. C
D.	7. C	**E.**	9. A		
	8. C		10. B		

COMBINED SKILLS: Test A

1. B		6. A
2. D		7. C
3. B		8. A
4. D		9. C
5. B		10. D

COMBINED SKILLS: Test B

1. C		6. D
2. B		7. A
3. D		8. B
4. C		9. A
5. B		10. D

COMBINED SKILLS: Test C

1. D		6. A
2. C		7. C
3. C		8. B
4. A		9. B
5. B		10. C

COMBINED SKILLS: Test D

1. B		6. D
2. A		7. T
3. C		8. A
4. A		9. D
5. B		10. D

Notes

Notes